Surfaces, Glazes & Firing

Surfaces, Glazes & Firing

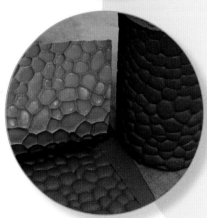

Angelica Pozo

LARK BOOKS

A Division of Sterling Publishing Co., Inc.
New York / London

EDITOR: Nathalie Mornu

COPY EDITOR: Carol Taylor

EDITORIAL ASSISTANT: Kathleen McCafferty

ART DIRECTOR: Thom Gaines

ART PRODUCTION ASSISTANT: Bradley Norris

PHOTOGRAPHERS: Dan Milner, principal

Steve Mann

Lynne Harty

ILLUSTRATOR: Orrin Lundgren

COVER DESIGNER: Celia Naranjo

COVER PHOTO: Tara Dawley,
Vase, 2009. Photo by artist

Library of Congress Cataloging-in-Publication Data

Pozo, Angelica.
  Ceramics for beginners : surfaces, glazes & firing / Angelica Pozo. -- 1st ed.
    p. cm.
  Includes index.
  ISBN 978-1-60059-245-4 (hc-plc with jacket : alk. paper)
  1. Glazes. 2. Pottery craft. I. Title.
  TT922.P693 2010
  738.1'4--dc22

                                        2009046013

10 9 8 7 6 5 4 3 2 1

First Edition

Published by Lark Books, A Division of
Sterling Publishing Co., Inc.
387 Park Avenue South, New York, NY 10016

Text © 2010, Angelica Pozo
Photography © 2010, Lark Books, A Division of Sterling Publishing Co., Inc.,
unless otherwise specified
Illustrations © 2010, Lark Books, A Division of Sterling Publishing Co., Inc.,
unless otherwise specified

Distributed in Canada by Sterling Publishing, c/o Canadian Manda Group,
165 Dufferin Street, Toronto, Ontario, Canada M6K 3H6

Distributed in the United Kingdom by GMC Distribution Services,
Castle Place, 166 High Street, Lewes, East Sussex, England BN7 1XU

Distributed in Australia by Capricorn Link (Australia) Pty Ltd.,
P.O. Box 704, Windsor, NSW 2756 Australia

If you have questions or comments about this book, please contact:
Lark Books
67 Broadway, Asheville, NC 28801
828-253-0467

Manufactured in China

ISBN 13: 978-1-60059-245-4

For information about custom editions, special sales, and premium and
corporate purchases, please contact the Sterling Special Sales Department at
800-805-5489 or specialsales@sterlingpub.com.

For information about desk and examination copies available to college and
university professors, submit requests to academic@larkbooks.com. Our
complete policy can be found at www.larkbooks.com.

Contents

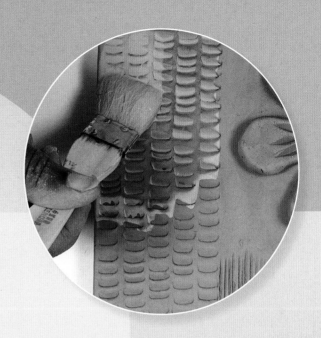

Introduction

As a child, I absolutely had to have the biggest crayon box they made, the one with 64 crayons in it. What if my drawing called for cornflower blue, and I didn't have it?! That just wouldn't do. Decorating ceramics is like having the biggest box of crayons ever.

Throughout my development as an artist, this same compulsion has followed me. I've always had to have the biggest set of materials available in any medium I got into, be it watercolor pencils or tempera paints. In my 36-year journey through the world of ceramics, I've sought out every form of surface decoration I could find. With every new technique or decorative trick I've discovered or mastered, my ceramic crayon box has gotten larger and more varied. And I'm happy to share with others.

■ ABOUT ME

While pursuing a BFA in painting, I took a ceramics class as an elective and switched majors on the spot. I went on to complete a BFA and MFA in ceramics, and have worked for 25 years as a full-time, self-employed ceramic artist, but I've never lost what painting taught me.

Back in that first ceramics class, my painter's eye saw similarities between ceramic decorating techniques and techniques for works on paper and canvas, but clay has them beat. That's because clay brings dimension and tactility—images you can touch and feel, forms you can hold and use. How could I not be smitten?

■ ABOUT THIS BOOK

First, what my book is not: a manual on forming and shaping clay. I assume you already know how to do that. (If you're new to making things out of clay, however, or need a refresher, there are good books available, including the first two in this Ceramics for Beginners series: *Hand Building* [Lark Books, 2008] and *Wheel Throwing* [Lark Books, 2010].) Instead, this book is about decorating the surface of clay: using color and texture, line and shape, pattern and image to transform an attractive form into an object of brilliant beauty.

We'll begin with an overview. Since clay can be decorated at every stage of the ceramic process—from wet ware and leather-hard, to greenware and bisque, to glaze firing and beyond—I'll review the ceramic process briefly, and describe the decorating techniques you can use at every stage. Next, I'll provide a bit of theory and lots of practical suggestions for translating your visual ideas into actual designs, and for developing those ideas in the first place. Getting Familiar with the Decorating Studio introduces the tools and materials that make decorating clay so much fun. (This is when you get to shop.) You'll also learn some basic skills, such as brushwork and transferring a design onto clay, as well as important safety tips.

Then comes the heart of the book: the techniques for decorating clay. Organized in the same order as the ceramic process, these techniques will soon have you carving and stamping; combing and drawing; staining and stenciling; glazing and overglazing; and much, much more. Finally, you'll find a discussion of the all-important topic of kilns and firing.

■ ABOUT YOU

You're probably not a professional ceramist, or even an expert. (People with that kind of knowledge hardly ever pick up a book entitled "For Beginners.") Perfect. This book is for you. The idea is to relax, have fun, and discover your own creativity through constructive play. Try the techniques on scraps of clay, or on an existing piece that you didn't like anyway. Even when you get around to the real thing, remember that nothing is forever. Carved surfaces can be smoothed and recarved, appliqués can be peeled off, underglaze can be scrubbed off, glazes can be reglazed. Right up until the first firing, your whole piece can be thrown into the clay bucket, melted back into clay, reclaimed, reworked, and made into something new. It's so much more forgiving than those crayon marks we all used to make.

My Project Tiles and Design Directive

In each technique chapter, I'll demonstrate the steps on a project tile, whose flat surface makes the process easy to see. Just for fun, I set myself a simple design directive: each project tile had to have a central floral image or motif, and a border or framing structure to accentuate the central image. Of course, I occasionally interpreted this directive loosely. But you should be able to see what diverse paths one simple design quest can take. So keep an eye out for the Design Considerations. You can follow along as I figure out how to make each composition work—and contemplate how you might have done it differently.

You'll also find Finishing Suggestions for each tile, indicating which glazes or finishes work especially well for each technique.

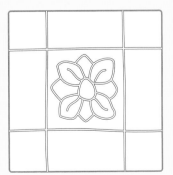

Decorating Clay: An Overview

The decorative potential of clay is endless. Ceramic surfaces can range from pure, simple, and utilitarian to richly brocaded with decorative adornment. They can act as flat or dimensional canvases for images that blur the boundaries between two- and three-dimensional space. They can even play chameleon, mimicking any other material you might want to simulate.

Chapter 5: carving at leather hard stage

Chapter 6: working with slip and wax resist at leather-hard stage

Chapter 5: impressing at wet ware stage

WHAT MAKES THIS VARIETY POSSIBLE is that decoration on clay can happen at all stages of the entire ceramic process, from wet clay through the glazed and fired stage and beyond. The two processes walk hand in hand. Let's begin with a brief review.

■ THE CERAMIC PROCESS

It all starts with clay—moist, pliable, fragrant with earth and possibility. When you have shaped and formed it into the object of your desire, it becomes *wet ware*.

As your ware begins the drying process, it will start to firm up a bit. It will become stiff and may crack if you try to bend it, but it will still be damp enough to carve and to accept attachments. This stage is called *leather hard*.

Once the ware dries completely, it's known as *greenware*. It will have lightened in color, and if it's held against your cheek, it will not feel damp. At this point the ware feels hard, but if you were to knock it a bit, it would chip or crumble. If you were to set it out in the rain, it would melt into a pile of clay mud.

Greenware is ready for the kiln. How you fire it may vary, depending on your decorating plans, but you will usually *bisque fire* it at a comparatively low temperature: 562°F to 1832°F

(294°C to 1000°C). Although this temperature is too low for the clay to completely mature, the bisque firing hardens the fragile greenware, leaving it porous and able to absorb glazes. It is now *bisque ware*.

The second, or *glaze*, firing generally occurs at higher temperatures and takes the glaze to its maturing temperature. When the clay is taken to its maturing temperature, it will have *vitrified*: It will be hard, durable, ceramic material. (For a thorough discussion of this process, see "The Science of Firing," page 116.)

■ THE DECORATION PROCESS

Every stage of the ceramic process offers unique opportunities for decoration.

From the moment the walls of your piece start going up and the form starts taking shape, decorating decisions need to be made. Do you want to keep the throwing rings—the ridged markings that your fingers left as they moved up the sides of the turning piece? Do you want the coils of construction to remain visible as a decorative texture, or do you want to smooth them out, providing a clean slate for other imagery or texture?

While still at the *wet ware* stage, the pliable surface of the clay can be textured with impressions and stamps, and built upon with appliqués and collagelike designs of colored clay.

As the ware moves into the *leather-hard* stage, incising and carving are possible, with their enormous scope for complex texture and relief imagery.

In the *wet ware* through *leather-hard* stages, slip decoration expands our options. Slip is merely a suspension of clay and water, but it can be combed and brushed into regular or irregular patterns. It can be squeezed from trailing bottles to leave raised lines across the surface. It can provide a base for *sgraffito*, which involves scratching a design through a layer of slip, revealing the color below. It gives us slip inlay, in which the decorative line is imbedded in the ceramic surface, for a more subtle effect.

You'll learn to make and use *terra sigillata*, a special kind of slip made only from the finest particles of clay. Similar to materials used by the ancient Greeks and Native Americans on their pottery, "terra sig" is applied to greenware or bisque ware and can be burnished with a river stone to a high sheen.

The *bisque* surface brings new materials into play. Underglaze in its many forms makes a complete drawing and painting kit: liquids for brushing; chalk, pen, and pencil for drawing and texturing.

Sponging, spattering, and spraying offer still more alternatives for interesting textural effects on smooth areas, while staining adds depth and contrast to areas that are already textured.

And then there are the glazes—the richest, most varied, most dramatic decorating materials, capable of producing the most gorgeous effects.

The decorative potential of clay is indeed endless, and available to both the expert and the beginner.

Chapter 6: sgraffito at leather-hard stage

Chapter 7: greenware and bisque

Chapter 8: bisque

Design and Inspiration

As exciting as decorating tools and materials may be, they're only that: tools and materials for accomplishing your creative purpose. To make them work for you, you'll need a design.

AT ITS SIMPLEST, the creative process is coming up with a solution to a visual design problem. There is no standardized checklist to follow. We must all seek out our own design quests and find our own way. The creative path is a very personal journey, and we walk it in the company of our own experiences and inclinations.

This can be liberating, but it can also leave you feeling a bit lost. Not to worry. Others have trod this path before, and they've left a few sign posts along the way.

■ THE DESIGN PROCESS

To design your ceramic work is to organize your ideas and experiences into a meaningful and cohesive visual statement embodied in clay. There are several ways to do this.

Some experienced artists visualize and plan their design completely and then execute it in clay, right down to the last detail. That's one valid approach. Others of us are more casual and intuitive, relying on action and reaction. We organize, rather than plan. This is probably a more accessible approach for the beginner—and, honestly, way more fun. The "ideal" approach may be a combination of the two: a bit of planning to get you started, then allowing your initial concept to take you where it will, organizing your ideas and components as you go along.

Whatever your approach, the Elements of Design (pages 11–13) and the Principles of Design (pages 14–16) will serve you well. They may sound theoretical, but they're purely practical, because *they help you see better.* They can take you from "this isn't working and I don't know why" all the way to "this design is confusing because nothing stands out as important, so I need to add some emphasis." There are six elements of design, which are governed by seven principles of design, and all 13 are your friends.

To figure out the value of a particular color, try matching it up to its place along a value scale.

■ THE ELEMENTS OF DESIGN

The basis of all visual language, the elements of design reside in every object we see around us. Whether the design is good or bad, whether the object is ugly or pleasing, it contains most, if not all, of these six elements.

Line. A line is a point that decided to take a walk. In addition to its obvious qualities of width, length, and direction, line also has focus and feeling: sharp or fuzzy, jagged or smooth. It can take on gestural, sketchy, or calligraphic personalities and help to set the mood of a composition.

A line can be an individual feature within the composition or serve to define shapes and contours. What's more, a line may be actually present or implied by the edge of a shape, by a grouping of objects, by the direction that an object is pointing, by the direction of a person's gaze. Grouped together, lines create a sense of value, density, or texture. **1**

Shape/Form. A shape is created when a line, actual or implied, crosses itself or intersects with other lines to enclose a space. A shape is two-dimensional, possessing height and width but no depth. A form, a three-dimensional element, has depth. The boundaries blur at times: for example, when a drawn shape is shaded and given the illusion of dimension.

A shape or form can be geometric—think circles, squares, and triangles for a shape; spheres, cones, cylinders, pyramids, and cubes for a form. A shape or form can also be *organic*. While that includes anything seen in nature, it also means free flowing, informal, and irregular. **2**

Value/Tone. Value and tone concern light and dark. Value represents the difference between black and white, and all the tones in between. A value scale (also known as a grey scale) is an evenly spaced charting of tones from white to black, as in photo 3.

Value also refers to the lightness or darkness of a color. Different hues fall at different points on a grey scale, with yellow being the lightest, purples and blues generally the darkest.

The value of a color can be changed by the addition of white, which is called a *tint*. A *shade* is a darker tone, made by adding black. Compositions are said to be in *high key*, if made up of all light values, or in *low key*, if they have only dark values. The best compositions have some value contrast, with light and dark used to create variety and interest. **3**

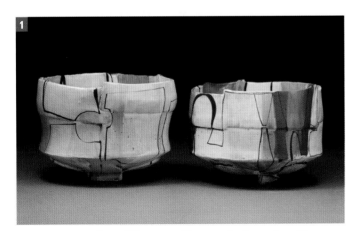

The lines that make up this composition vary in size and quality, creating interest. Color and value also play key roles. Kari Smith, *Bowls*, 2009. 6 x 16 x 8 inches (15.2 x 40.6 x 20.3 cm). Hand-built red clay; grolleg slip; hand-painted commercial engobes; electric fired; cone 6. Photo by artist

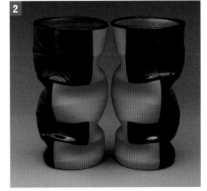

Playing visual tricks with shape and form. While clearly an image of two three-dimensional forms, the contrast of the gloss against the matt orange glaze leads us to connect the flat matt areas into one flat shape. George Bowes, *Tumblers: Secondary*, 2007. Each, 6½ x 3½ inches (16.5 x 8.9 cm). Thrown and altered porcelain; underglazes; glazes; cone 5. Photo by artist

Color. Color can be a powerful design tool, eliciting strong emotional and psychological responses. It is characterized by hue, value, and saturation. A color's *hue* is its position on the visible spectrum or color wheel: red, blue, yellow, or green, for example. Its *value* is its lightness or darkness (see above), and the *saturation* is its intensity. The more grey a color has in it, the less saturated, the less pure it is.

The 12 basic hues are organized by a color wheel into three categories: the *primary colors* of red, blue, and yellow; the *secondary colors* of orange, violet, and green; and the *intermediary*, or *tertiary*, colors of red orange, yellow green, red violet, blue violet, blue green, and yellow orange. **4**

When you combine different colors, you begin to create color relationships, or *harmonies*. There are various kinds of harmonies, and they can help in choosing colors. If you like green, for instance, but don't know what else to combine with it, simply find green's partner or partners in one of the following color harmonies, until you come up with a combination that works for you.

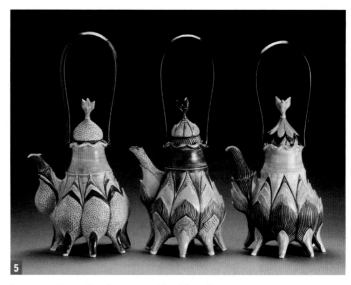

5

Incorporating colors from opposite sides of the color wheel makes for a lively composition.
Jenny Lou Sherburne, *Three Lotus Teapots*, 2007. 18 x 8½ x 7 inches (45.7 x 21.6 x 17.8 cm). Wheel-thrown and pinched stoneware; appliquéd, carved; electric fired with slip, cone 05; glazes, cone 5–6. Photo by Tom Mills

4

Like paint colors, glaze and clay colors can be matched to their corresponding color family and used in color harmonies.

Complementary colors are two colors that fall opposite each other on the color wheel, creating a contrasting harmony—for example, green and red. A variation would be a split-complementary color scheme, which employs the colors adjacent to one of the complementary pairs. Continuing with green as our example, a split-complementary relationship would be green, red violet, and red orange. Once you've selected your scheme, the colors in that group can be used in tinted, shaded, saturated, or desaturated form. **5**

Analogous color schemes are more unified and harmonious. Analogous colors are next to each other on the color wheel: for example, red, red orange, and orange. **6** **7**

Triadic harmony uses three equally spaced colors on the color wheel: for example, yellow, red, and blue; or green, orange, and violet. Triadic harmonies offer balance.

Monochromatic harmony involves only one hue used in different values and intensities. This kind of color scheme can unify a composition.

Colors are also distinguished by *temperature*. *Warm colors*—red, orange, and yellow, the colors of fire—give a feeling of warmth. Cool colors imply coolness: blue and violet, for example, the colors of water, and green, the color of cool grass.

To make these concepts meaningful and personal, take a look at your wardrobe, your home, the artwork you covet or collect. Is there a recurring choice of colors or type of color harmony? Do you lean toward cool or warm colors? Perhaps you see a preference for those energizing complementary color combinations. Or perhaps the more harmonious, analogous color combination are at play. Once you see what surrounds you, you may decide to expand upon those preferences or (who knows?) bring out a hidden side of your personality.

Texture/Pattern. One of the most alluring aspects of a ceramic piece is how welcoming it is to the touch, how it feels in your hand. Texture is important in ceramics. There are two kinds of texture in art. *Physical*, or *tactile*, refers to the actual texture of the surface: rough or smooth, hard and glassy. In ceramics, physical texture includes the feel of the glaze or the unglazed clay, as well as the pressed, stamped, or incised markings on the surface.

Visual, or *implied*, texture is not felt, but seen: a crackle glaze, for example, or one with iron

6

Utilizing colors closest to each other on the color wheel helps create a pleasing, calming effect. Used here are green, saturated and desaturated, and blue green. Neil Patterson, *Three Large Candlestick Pairs*, 2008. 11 x 5 x 5 inches (27.9 x 12.7 x 12.7 cm). Wheel-thrown, altered, faceted, and assembled white stoneware; electric fired; cone 6. Photo by artist.

7

Colors from the outer ends of an analogous color group can inject a bit of visual energy into a predominantly harmonious composition. Neil Patterson, *Condiment Bowls Enshrined*, 2009. 10 x 12 x 8 inches (25.4 x 30.5 x 20.3 cm). Wheel-thrown, altered, and assembled white stoneware; electric fired; cone 6. Photo by artist.

spotting or interesting speckling. The techniques of sponging and spattering (see page 88) create visual texture, as do painted or drawn patterns. **8**

Space/Depth. Space refers to the three-dimensionality of a form or sculpture. There's *positive space*, the space the piece itself takes up, and *negative space*, the space around a form, or the space inside a vessel.

Depth refers to the illusion of space in a two-dimensional image. You can create depth on the surface of your form by playing with value, color, and pattern. Depth can also refer to layers of decorative treatment visible on the surface. **9**

The crater glaze and imbedded wires provide the form with physical texture, which contrasts with the smooth surface of the satin matt glaze. The golden flecks among the green add visual texture to a physically smooth surface. Todd Leech, *Circuit*, 2009. 7 x 4¼ x 2½ inches (17.8 x 10.8 x 6.4 cm). Hand-built stoneware; drilled, kiln elements added; foaming and reaching glaze, barium matte glaze; gas kiln fired; cone 10; drilled holes selectively reopened with screwdriver. Photo by artist

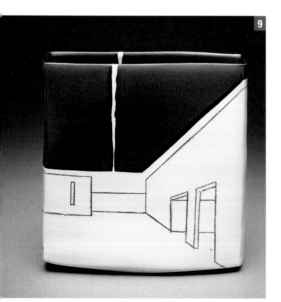

Creating the illusion of deep space on a rather narrow form. Maren Kloppmann, *Envelope Vase with Drawing*, 2007. 8½ x 8 x 2 inches (21.6 x 20.3 x 5.1 cm). Wheel-thrown and altered porcelain; wax resist, drawing; glaze, underglaze pencil; electric fired; cone 9. Photo by Peter Lee

■ PRINCIPLES OF DESIGN

The principles govern the relationship of the design elements and organize the composition as a whole. How you apply the principles of design will determine how successful the design will be.

Balance. A balanced design appears stable; it conveys a sense of wholeness and equilibrium. Balance can be symmetrical and evenly balanced, or asymmetrical and unevenly balanced. In general, asymmetrical compositions have a greater sense of visual tension. **10**

Asymmetrical compositions tend to have a greater sense of visual tension. Ruchika Madan, Food Chain: *Fish and Roe*, 2009. 9 x 6 x 1 inches (22.9 x 15.2 x 2.5 cm). Slab-built and hump-molded white stoneware; slip decorated, paper stencil; sgraffito, trailing; gloss and matte glazes; cone 6, oxidation. Photo by artist.

Contrast/Variety. Contrast, or variety, is the juxtaposition of opposing elements, such as a rough texture with a smooth surface, light against dark, or the use of complementary colors. Contrast can define a composition, helping to delineate the difference between shapes. Contrast can also be used as a background, to bring objects forward in a design. It can create an area of emphasis, adding visual discord and interest. **11**

Emphasis. Emphasis, or dominance, gives an element visual prominence. Attention is drawn to an area, or focal point, making it more important than the other elements in the composition. Emphasis can be established through contrasting values, colors, size, or placement within the composition. **12**

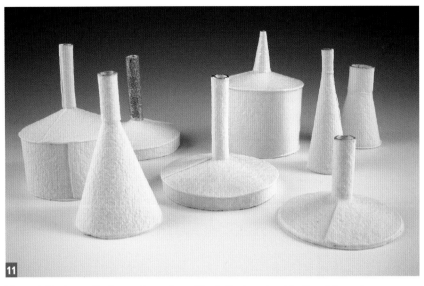

The gold luster on the lips and spout provide distinct contrast to the white, pulp-textured surfaces of these vessels. Billie Jean Theide, *Almost White: Oils*, 2007. 3½ x 10 x 8 inches (8.9 x 25.4 x 20.3 cm). Porcelain; cone 13; gas reduction; clear glaze; cone 13 gas reduction; 22-karat gold luster; electric fired; cone 018. Photo by artist

Contrasting textures, tones, and colors help draw our eye to the focal point of this composition, the area of the branch-like image. Jeff Reich, *The Insistence of Thorns*, 2009. 14 x 14 x ¾ inches (16 x 16 x 1.9 cm). Hand-built black stoneware; reduction fired; cone 10; glaze sgraffito, crawling, shino glaze; cone 06, Mayco red fired to cone 10. Photo by artist.

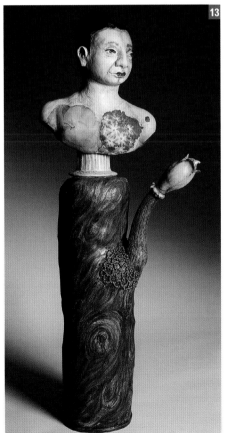

Movement. Movement is the visual flow through or around a composition, as your eye is directed from one place to another. Variations in shapes, lines, and curves can suggest motion, as do carefully placed areas of light and dark. Diagonal lines create the illusion of movement. Similar shapes connected with each other, or beside each other, can imply restlessness. **13**

The diagonally angled, swirling texture and the slightly askew posture of the figure work together to create a sense of movement throughout the piece. Matt Nolen, *Mating Season Meant a Change of Color for Simon*, 2009. 36 x 14 x 8 inches (91.4 x 35.6 x 20.3 cm). Hand-built white stoneware; slips, stains and underglaze decoration; cone 6 glaze, electric kiln; refired to cone 04 for laser-print transfers; china paint, luster; decals fired to cone 018. Photo by Caryn Leigh Posnansky

Scale/Proportion. Scale refers to the size of an object relative to its environment, to the human body, to its form, or to its function, as well as the proportion of its own components to each other. Exaggerated size can be used to create emphasis. **14**

Rhythm/Repetition. Rhythm is a repetition or alternation of elements within a overall design. It can create a sense of movement, as well as establishing pattern and texture. Without some variation, repetition can become monotonous. **15**

Unity/Harmony. Unity or harmony exists when all the elements in the composition work together in an amicable fashion. Unity helps to visually organize a form or composition, facilitating interpretation and understanding. **16**

In this composition, several distinct elements repeat at different intervals, creating a symphony of rhythms. Posey Bacopoulos, *Hexagonal Bowl*, 2007. 3 x 15 x 14 (7.6 x 38.1 x 35.6 cm). Slab-built and textured terra-cotta; majolica with painted stains, sgraffito; electric fired, cone 04. Photo by Kevin Nobel.

Exaggerated scale can make an artistic statement. Kristen Cliffel, *Say, I Do*, 2007. 24 x 17 x 17 inches (61 x 43.2 x 43.2 cm). Hand-built low-fire clay and glaze, cone 05; multiple firings; resin. Photo by artist.

Though the tray is very colorful and every bowl is a different color, the repeated use of seafoam green glaze unites these unique elements into a set. Susan DeMay, *Color Studies in the Round*, 2005. 23 x 12¼ x 1¾ inches (58.4 x 31.1 x 4.4 cm). Slab-built and press-molded stoneware; tape and wax resist; cone 6 glazes; electric fired, cone 6. Photo by John Lucas.

Take note of interesting surfaces in the natural and manmade world around you. Photograph them so that later, in the studio, you can figure out how to translate them into ceramic decoration. Todd Leech, *Stryke*, 2008. 22 x 14 x 9 inches (55.9 x 35.6 x 22.9 cm). Hand-built stoneware; drilled with kiln elements in center hole; foaming and reaching glaze; gas kiln, cone 10; drilled holes selectively reopened with screwdriver. Photos by artist.

Todd Leech
Train Boxcar, 2008.

■ FINDING INSPIRATION

Inspiration is all around us, all the time. We just need to pay attention.

Train your eyes to notice the intriguing texture on the side of a decaying building; the lyrical line of a seedpod; the yummy color combinations in the clothing of a crowd of strangers. Take note of what visually resonates with you. Photograph it, sketch it, flag that page in the book, or at least try to remember what caught your eye and held your fascination. Incorporate your daily visual discoveries into your own personal visual vocabulary. Look at the work that others have created, and how they solved their design challenges. Use your sketchbook to create a visual *dictionary*: your personal vocabulary of the things you find visually interesting. It will be yours to reference in the future.

Train your hands to remember the experiences that made a strong impression on them. Many ideas for artistic work spring directly from the experience of working with your hands, with the clay, with the decorating materials. The more you put your hands to work, the more creative discoveries you'll find.

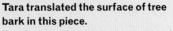

Tara translated the surface of tree bark in this piece.
Tara Dawley, *Vase*, 2009. 12 x 11 x 11 inches (30.5 x 27.9 x 27.9 cm). Wheel-thrown stoneware; carved; glazes; gas reduction, cone 10. Photos by artist.

Look at your collections, or begin to collect items that you find of interest. With the object right in front of you, you can easily begin to incorporate elements of its form or surface into your work. **Farraday Newsom** painted her dishware with motifs based on natural objects. **Frank James Fisher**, on the other hand, models his work directly from oil cans; can you tell which ones are real, and which he's made? Frank James Fisher, *Tea Can*, 2009. 5½ x 5 x 7 inches (14 x 12.7 x 17.8 cm). Wheel-thrown and hand-built porcelain; bisque; cone 06 glaze; raku fired twice; reduction; wire bail; mask, sponge clay, washes, scrubbed-off glaze, splatter. Photo by artist.

Farraday Newsome, *Lushness and Grace Place Setting*, 2007. Setting, 5 x 12 x 12 (12.7 x 30.5 x 30.5 cm); cup, 4 x 4 x 3 inches (10.2 x 10.2 x 7.6 cm). Hand-built terra-cotta; electric fired, cone 1; brushed colored glazes on white majolica base glaze, cone 05. Photos by artist.

If you've enjoyed making art in another medium, consider how to reapply your strengths in it (or your affection for it) into clay work. **Kathy King incorporates the types of marks she makes while carving printmaking blocks into her clay work.** Kathy King, Untitled, 2008. 12 x 12 x 1 inches (30.5 x 30.5 x 2.5 cm). Wheel-thrown cone 6 porcelain; sgraffito carved; clear glaze; cone 6 oxidation fired. Photos by artist.

■ GETTING STARTED

Ideas spring from inspiration. If you surround yourself with plenty of inspiration, if you allow yourself to play with clay, ideas will come.

So lose the need to make the perfect piece. Embrace a world of discovery, experimentation, and enjoyment. The best creative discoveries are the ones that surprise you while you're having fun.

Most important, if you're struggling with a design decision, remember that there are a million right answers, not just one. Your task is to find the ones that work for you.

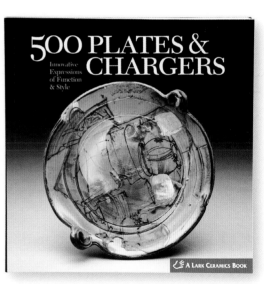

There are so many ways to find inspiration. Look at the work of other artists, handle it if you can so as to see all sides, and note how they shaped and decorated the kinds of forms you're aiming to make. Or flip through books and magazines to see photos of many different pieces and styles.

Getting Familiar with the Decorating Studio

Aesthetically attuned and filled with inspiration, you're probably ready to get your hands dirty. Almost! Browse this chapter first. You'll find a few safety tips; the tools you'll want to adapt or buy; the materials that will make your clay pieces sing; and a few basic techniques that will serve you well.

■ SAFETY

Surface decoration brings its own set of safety concerns, in addition to those of general clay work. By following the simple guidelines described below, you can make decorating both safe and rewarding.

Material Safety

Dust, our biggest health issue in clay work, can be an even greater concern in some decorating applications. You may be aware of the threat of silicosis, a lung disease caused by the inhalation of silica, a major ingredient in clay and a significant ingredient in many decorating materials. Additionally, decorating materials have other ingredients for

fluxing (melting) and coloring that may include heavy metals, for which contact should be limited, and toxic materials, for which contact should be avoided altogether. So pay keen attention to the materials that you plan to use. Read the labels carefully and do your research on any bulk dry materials you decide to handle.

These days, because of government safety laws, many commercial decorating materials are clearly labeled nontoxic, lead-free, and/or dinnerware-safe. It's a selling point, so if the label doesn't make the claim, the claim probably can't be made. A responsible company will also warn on their labeling

if the product contains any kind of toxic materials. If information is lacking on the package, ask your merchant. Also check the company's website; look for product specifications or request them. If you find no health information about the product, handle it as possibly toxic and definitely not dinnerware-safe.

By law, a product labeled *nontoxic* is safe to ingest accidentally and therefore safe to use with young children. *Not dinnerware-safe* simply means that, when fired, this material doesn't produce a surface that's suitable to eat from; the material itself may or may not be toxic. Check for additional notations on toxicity.

Safe Work Habits

When working with toxins, physical contact needs to be avoided as much as the inhalation of their dust. If you find yourself working with toxic materials, wear rubber or vinyl gloves as you glaze and handle your work, as well as a dust mask. Toxic materials should be respected.

Keep your studio or workspace clean, to avoid kicking dust up into the air as you move around. When dust can't be avoided—when you're working with dusty materials, say, or scraping or sanding your piece—wearing a dust mask or respirator is vital.

Safety Checklist

☐ **KEEP IT CLEAN.** Start with a clean working environment; clean up immediately after spillages and after you're done. To keep dust down, wet wiping or mopping is a better practice than brushing or sweeping.

☐ **KEEP IT SEPARATE.** Do not eat, drink, or smoke while working, to avoid ingestion of unsafe materials.

☐ **KEEP IT HEALTHY.** Wear a respirator when creating or kicking up dust, or when working with dusty materials.

☐ **KEEP IT SAFE.** Wear rubber or vinyl gloves when working with hazardous materials. The safest thing to do is avoid using toxic materials in the first place.

■ TOOLS OF THE TRADE

In any craft, tools are part of the fun. For this one you'll need some basic studio equipment, a lot of decorating tools, and a couple of ways to keep track of your ideas and your experiments.

Basic Studio Equipment

▼ **A paper dust mask** can be found at the local hardware store. It's good to wear when sanding greenware or adding water to a small batch of dry, nontoxic materials.

▼ **A respirator** is a must if you mix your own glazes or clay bodies from dry materials. Whether they're toxic or not, prolonged exposure to any dust can cause serious lung ailments.

▼ **Gloves** made of latex or vinyl should be worn whenever your hands will be exposed to or immersed in toxic materials. While lead is clearly a toxin, many coloring oxides are made up of heavy metals, to which you should limit your exposure.

▼ **An apron** is a good way to keep your clothes clean and avoid tracking residue from the studio into your living quarters.

◀ **Spray bottles** are handy for keeping your clay moist enough while you decorate it at the wet to leather-hard stages. Spray bottles can even be used to create some decorative effects. You might want to have a separate one to spray decorating materials, so as not to accidently contaminate your wet work.

▲ **Plastic buckets and containers with tight lids**, both large and small, provide excellent storage for your decorating materials, because they're nonreactive and airtight. Metal lids or metal containers may rust or corrode, so don't use them for slips and glazes.

▶ **A banding wheel** (think lazy Susan on a pedestal) allows you to view your ware easily from all sides. It's especially handy when working on vertical pieces; as the piece turns, you can see how the decoration flows.

Decorating Tools

You may well have some of these in your clay toolbox already. There are specialized decorating tools available that are a delight to use, but many can be improvised. I'll show you both, so you can get to work right away and take your time to accumulate the rest.

▼ **A pony or pastry roller**, available at both ceramic supply shops and houseware departments, is basically a mini rolling pin that you can use with one hand. A printmaking brayer will also work. A regular-size rolling pin will be handy with some techniques.

▼ **Incising and carving tools** are used in quite a few techniques. Needle tools, loop tools, and a ball stylus will do the job. It's good to have an array of tools that can create a variety of thick and thin incised and carved lines.

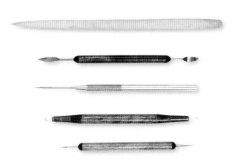

▲ **Modeling tools** can be made of wood from end to end, but the most versatile are rubber-tipped. They're useful for compressing, smoothing, and getting into tight spots. They're also great for incising into moist clay. Each provides a different line quality, from the hard, crisp-edged line of the wooden variety to the soft, responsive, more organic lines of a rubber-tipped tool. The latter are also useful for manipulating decorating materials at later stages of clay work.

◀ **Ribs,** used primarily to shape and smooth clay walls, come in a variety of materials. For decorative purposes, you'll need a stiff rubber rib and a metal one.

▼ **Texturing tools** can include a broad variety of toothed or serrated ceramic tools, as well as found and reappropriated objects.

◄ **Burnishing tools** are used to compress and buff a smooth, specially coated ceramic surface to produce a sheen. A piece of chamois will create a soft sheen; a smooth, round stone or the back of a spoon can result in a high gloss.

► **Sponges** of different sizes and varieties are useful for a spectrum of applications. You'll need a big household one for cleaning up your workspace and a few others for decorating. Synthetic sponges are good for wiping excess decorating material off of ware when staining, natural ones are good for sponging on textural decoration, and pop-up sponges can become decorative stamps.

► **Brushes** are among the most widely used decorating tools, so it's best to have a good selection of shapes, styles, and sizes. From the small liner brush to the broad, flat hake brush, those with soft, natural hairs generally give smoother results, especially with slip and glaze. Oriental brushes are a good choice. They're full-bodied, hold a lot of material, are available at economical prices, and the round ones keep a good point. Synthetic, sablelike brushes work very well with underglazes, especially with more detailed work.

Stencil brushes make crisp and tidy stenciled images.

Hake brushes are excellent for applying a good, even coat.

For spattering, flicking a toothbrush with your thumb works very well, but spatter brushes can do the job more quickly and evenly.

Synthetic watercolor brushes work great with underglazes, producing smooth, even applications.

Dagger brushes are especially good in majolica for making fluid lines that vary from thick to thin.

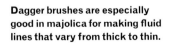

A fan brush creates textured and feathered effects.

Mop brushes hold a lot of material, making them good for brushing generous layers of slips and glazes.

Oriental brushes are the workhorses of ceramic brushes and are often a good buy. Their soft yet springy bristles hold up to expressive painterly approaches with slip, glazes, underglazes, and majolica colors.

▼ **Slip- and glaze-trailing tools**, available in a variety of styles and sizes, are used to draw raised lines with slip or glaze. Detachable pen nibs of different sizes are available for many of them, enabling you to do detailed fine line drawings with underglaze.

◀ **A mechanical mouth atomizer** is an inexpensive apparatus used to spray stains or underglazes onto your work. Available in a couple of different styles, they reduce liquid to a fine spray.

▼ **Glaze dipping tongs** are used to grasp ceramic ware firmly but with minimal contact, allowing you to dip the entire piece in a bucket of glaze and remove it entirely glazed, with no marks or fingerprints.

Recording Tools

Creative ideas can pop up just about anywhere, anytime. If you don't record them, you'll lose them! A sketchbook about 9 x 12 inches (22.9 x 30.5 cm) gives you plenty of room for a fast doodle or a quick sketch, along with your notes and any photos or clippings you'd like to attach.

Another use for that sketchbook is keeping a glaze journal. You'll want to remember what worked and what didn't. As you glaze a piece, do a quick sketch, noting the process, the order of all the steps, and the materials and colors used. If you're working production style, with several identical pieces that have different glazing, label the bottom of the pieces so you'll be able to match them to their glazing notes later.

You'll of course need pencils and erasers, but a pad of tracing paper and perhaps a colored pencil set will also come in handy. Other drawing aids such as rulers, compasses, and triangles can be quite useful, as well as scissors, masking tape, and paste.

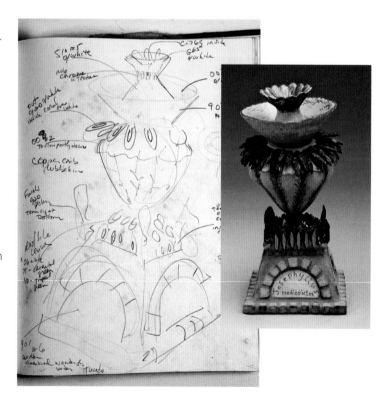

■ MATERIALS

Now that you've stocked your toolbox, it's time to collect your clay and the exciting materials that will decorate it.

Clay and Clay Bodies

Clay is your most important material, the foundation of ceramics—one simple substance with so many complexities. You're probably familiar with clay, but it would be helpful to review the characteristics that interact so intimately with decorating techniques.

RAW CLAY. Clay fresh from the riverbank isn't ready for ceramics. Some freshly mined clays are too sticky, without the physical strength needed to build larger pieces; they need coarser materials added to them. Others aren't sticky enough. They may be too coarse, lacking plasticity—that is, elasticity and pliability. They're likely to crack as you bend and shape them. To make them more workable, these clays benefit from the addition of stickier, or more plastic, clays.

CLAY BODIES. Such mixtures and additions create a *clay body,* the actual clay you purchase and use. The recipe for any given clay body may include several different clays, as well as several nonclay materials, all for the purpose of creating a clay with the properties necessary for its intended use. Clay body types are categorized primarily by firing temperature or specialized use. Common ones include earthenware, stoneware, porcelain, and raku clay.

One common addition is grog, ground-up particles of high-temperature, fired clay. Grog adds texture, strength, and workability, especially useful in sculpture, hand building, and tile making.

The individual recipe also determines the clay's firing temperature range. Each kind of ceramic clay, and every ingredient added to it, has a specific melting point; taken together, they determine the firing temperature at which the clay matures, or *vitrifies*—becomes hard, tight, durable ceramic material.

Along with many other factors, the kind of decorative effect you want can affect the clay body you choose. For example, if you plan to create fine,

delicate images, you'll want a smoother clay. If you're after a more rugged look, you may prefer a coarser clay. Choice of clay, in turn, affects choice of glaze, because the interaction between clay and glaze is critical. When it's fired, a glaze becomes a layer of glass that fuses to the surface of the clay. During and after the firing, each clay and each glaze has its own rate of expansion and contraction. If the rates don't match closely enough, various glaze defects or failures can occur. (Glaze defects are described on pages 98-99.)

Decorating Materials

Just as a painter has a multitude of mediums, a ceramic decorator has a plethora of choices as well.

▼ **Coloring oxides** are raw ceramic materials used to impart color to glazes, slips, and clay bodies. Sold in powdered form, they are mixed with water. They can be used as a wash, for brushed-on decoration, or to stain or patina a textured bisque surface.

▼ **A stain** is a stable coloring agent made up of one or more coloring oxides together with alumina, flint, and a fluxing compound to help it melt. Use stains to color glazes, overglazes, underglazes, and clay bodies. As with coloring oxides, washes may be made of stains as well and used to paint over a raw glaze in a decorating technique known as *majolica* (see page 100).

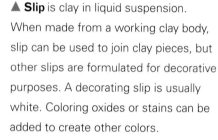

Depending on the clay body, slips can be used to join pieces or for decorative purposes.

▲ **Slip** is clay in liquid suspension. When made from a working clay body, slip can be used to join clay pieces, but other slips are formulated for decorative purposes. A decorating slip is usually white. Coloring oxides or stains can be added to create other colors.

Slips are formulated for specific stages of clay work. Wet ware slip formulas generally work on wet through leather-hard clay; other recipes are designed for greenware, and still others are formulated for bisque ware.

Engobe is another name for a decorating slip, though the term is often associated with a decorating material that's a hybrid of a slip and a glaze, more like a vitreous slip—one with enough flux to provide a durable surface with saturated color.

Slips are available commercially in dry mixed form. Many pottery shops will recommend one of their liquid casting slips—the ones poured into plaster molds to form those cute cast figures you see in ceramic hobby shops—as suitable for decorative purposes, but test before you use. Not all will work.

▼ **Underglazes** are colored decoration materials that are applied to bisque or greenware. Many need a covering glaze before final firing to intensify their color. However, there are vitreous underglazes that can stand on their own. Most underglazes are opaque, though many manufactures also offer an underglaze series that can be used as a translucent decorating material for watercolor-like effects or details, as well as an opaque color, depending upon the number of coats applied.

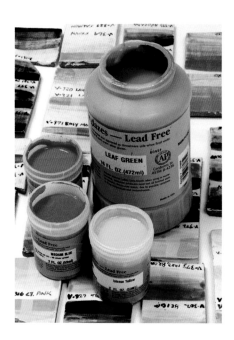

▼ **Glazes**, generally the finishing coat, come in the widest assortment of colors, surfaces, and characteristics. Like clay bodies, glazes are formulations of dry chemicals that impart different qualities to the glaze, including the temperature range at which it melts and achieves its optimum visual and physical attributes. Ready-to-use commercial glazes are widely available for earthenware as well as midrange stoneware temperatures. It's critical that the glaze be compatible with the clay body. A glaze that fires lower than the clay body will usually work fine, but never fire ware to higher than the rating of the clay it is made from, or you might open your kiln to find a melted pool of sludge.

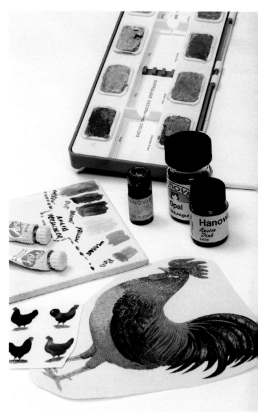

▲ **Overglaze** decorating materials are generally applied on top of a fired glaze surface and then refired to a very low temperature, ranging from cone 022 to cone 015. They include china paints, lusters, and decals.

◄ **Wax resist** is an emulsified (liquid) wax, available from ceramic supply houses. It's applied to ware prior to decorating to prevent slips, glazes, or underglazes from adhering to areas where you don't want them. Some are even tinted, so you can easily see where they've been applied. The tint comes in handy in decorative applications. The wax burns away during firing.

Commercial versus Homemade Decorating Materials

No contest. Commercial products are more convenient, more reliable, more stable, and more consistent in results—by far. Many professional ceramic artists, myself included, rely on commercial products for many of their decorating needs. Slips, underglazes, and glazes are all available in ready-to-use or just-add-water form, in a huge selection of colors and surfaces. There isn't much that can't be found.

I strongly recommend that beginners, especially those learning alone at home, use store-bought until they're more confident with their decorating abilities—that is, until they're no longer beginners. For that reason, commercial decorating materials have been used throughout the book, whenever possible. You may very well find that commercial products offer all you'll ever need. However, in case you're curious about the process, I've included a brief overview on page 122, along with a few recipes.

A huge variety of commercial glazes are available. Although glaze charts are valuable, glazes should be tested on test tiles before they're applied to your ware.

■ ESSENTIAL TECHNIQUES

Before we get to the specific techniques that comprise most of the book, let's get a few basic ones on the worktable.

Making Test Tiles

As I've said several times before—and will say several times again—clay chemistry is unpredictable. The best thing you can do for yourself is to find out how your decorating materials will interact with your clay body *before* your elegant vase emerges from the kiln as a pile of blistered, blackened shards.

Enter the test tile. You should test your decorating materials—glazes, underglazes, slips—on every new clay body recipe that you use. Don't assume that what worked on one will work on the other. Go ahead: Make your test tiles.

1 Roll out a slab of your clay body and cut it into strips, alternating wider and narrower strips. Set the wide strips upright on the narrower ones, to create a base for the tiles to stand on. (Don't forget to score and slip the strips before attaching them.) Upright tiles will tell you whether—and how—your materials will run on vertical forms.

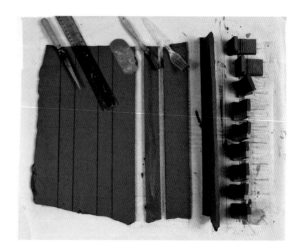

2 Let the strips firm up a bit to barely leather hard, then carve a band of grooves across the lower part of the whole strip to create some texture. A single swipe with a fork works really well. This will tell you how a glaze will work on a textured surface.

3 Cut the joined strips into tiles. Once cut, apply a contrasting wet ware slip now (or an underglaze later) so you can test the *transmittance* qualities of the glaze. Here I've used white slip for the red clay. A black slip would be a good choice for a white clay. (See "Working with Glazes," page 96.)

4 Allow to dry. Bisque fire the tiles, and set them aside until needed.

It's convenient to make the tiles as you shape your piece from the wet clay. Then you can bisque fire the tiles and the piece in the same firing.

Applying glaze to a bisqued test tile. The band of white slip along the edge helps test the transmittance of the glaze.

Compare the three test tiles on the left, made from the red clay body behind them, with the three tiles on the right, made from the white low-fire clay. Starting from the middle tiles and working outward, the tiles are greenware, bisque ware, and glazed with the same glaze. Note how widely the results differ with the two clays.

Transferring a Design to Clay

If you've developed an idea into a plan drawing, or found a copyright-free image that you'd like to use, there are several options for transferring some guidelines onto your piece, at different stages of clay work.

Transferring to Wet or Leather-Hard Clay

You'll need a piece of clear, heavy-weight (4 mil) plastic, a fine-tipped permanent marker, and a ball stylus or ball-point pen.

1 Tape your plan drawing onto your worktable. On top of it, tape a piece of the clear plastic large enough to cover it.

2 With the permanent marker, trace the major lines of your design onto the plastic. That plastic sheet can now be used repeatedly to transfer the guidelines for your image onto your work.

3 To transfer the drawing to your piece, lightly mist the clay so the plastic will stick to it, and position the image where you want it. Use the

stylus or ball-point pen to trace over your lines, lightly impressing guidelines into the clay. Lift off the plastic, and proceed with your decorating technique of choice.

Transferring to Bisque Ware

When planning out your decoration for bisque, you can draw directly onto the piece with a soft pencil. However, if freehand drawing isn't your forte or your image is a bit detailed, you can transfer your guidelines instead.

Plan A. If you're using your image only once or twice, this is the most direct approach. In addition to an old ball-point pen, you'll need tracing paper and graphite or transfer paper. There's also a nifty red transfer paper specially formulated for ceramics.

▶ **Tip:** If you're feeling especially frugal, you can make your own graphite paper by darkening one side of a piece of tracing paper with a dark-leaded pencil.

1 Trace your plan drawing onto a piece of tracing paper.

2 Position the traced drawing over your bisque piece and tape it in place. Slide a piece of graphite or transfer paper under it—graphite side toward the piece—and trace over the lines in the drawing with a blunt tool, such as a worn-out ball-point pen.

Check to see that you're actually making visible lines. If the graphite lines are too subtle, then invest in the ceramics transfer paper, which leaves clear red lines that later burn away in the firing.

Plan B. If you want to transfer an image numerous times, there's a timesaving technique called *pouncing*. It's not worth the trouble for just a couple of uses. You'll need tracing paper, cardboard, a straight pin, tape, a soft mop brush, and powdered graphite.

1 Trace your drawing onto tracing paper.

2 Lay the traced drawing over a piece of cardboard, and use a straight pin to make small perforations along all the lines.

3 Position the drawing on your piece, and tape it in place.

4 Dip a soft mop brush into powdered graphite, and use gentle, circular motions to work the graphite over the entire drawing.

5 Lift the paper, and your image is transferred. The graphite is very loose and dusty on the surface, so be careful not to smudge your guidelines away as you work or go over it with pencil.

■ BASIC APPLICATION METHODS

Multistem hake brushes are inexpensive and versatile; a wide one can be cut down to the size needed. Their soft, full hairs make them perfect for applying large areas of slip or homemade glaze.

Brushing

For slip and for most commercial glazes, brush application is the best technique for achieving a solid, even coating. For one thing, it doesn't use as much glaze as pouring and dipping. But mostly, it's simple and direct.

1 Mix the slip or glaze thoroughly, dissolving any lumps, and bring it to the right consistency—smooth pancake batter is a reliable benchmark. Add water if necessary.

2 Select the right brush. It should be made of soft hair and able to hold a lot of fluid. It should also be the right size for the task at hand: Use a broad, flat brush for large areas, and a brush with a good point for tighter spaces. (See "Brushes," page 23.)

3 Refrain from dragging the brush back and forth in a scrubbing motion, as if you were painting a house. You'll get a scratchy application that accentuates your brush strokes. Instead, hold a brush full of glaze or slip over the ware, and let just the tip of the brush hairs touch. The idea is to let the glaze flow from the brush onto your work. You need only move your brush around, directing where you want the flow to go.

4 Properly applied, slips usually get enough coverage in one coat. Most glazes need two or three. Allow each coat to dry before applying the next, and alternate your pattern or direction of movement with each coat.

Soft, synthetic, nylon-haired brushes are good choices for applying commercial glazes.

Studio Glazes

Studio-mixed glazes are a different story altogether. Some homemade glazes, especially high-fire ones, aren't at all suitable for brushing. They don't flow well during the firing and show all too well the subtleties of application, including brush marks. Even studio glazes suitable for brushing need a little help from additives, such as gum solution, to improve their physical flow and brushability. Gum solution is commercially available from ceramic suppliers as a liquid, or you can mix your own from a natural gum powder. (See "Recipes," page 122.)

Dipping

Dipping is a quick and efficient way to glaze a lot of ware. On the other hand, it requires a lot of glaze. (Slip can be applied by dipping or pouring, but these techniques are more common with glaze.)

1 A dipping glaze should be a bit thinner than a brushing one—about the consistency of buttermilk.

2 Prepare enough glaze so that you can immerse the entire piece; otherwise, you'll have to do first one side and then the other, and the glaze will be thicker where the applications overlap. With some glazes this may not make much of a difference, but with

others, the color could significantly change in the areas where the glaze is thicker.

3 It can be a challenge to hold the ware securely without marring the glaze. Happily, our nifty glaze-dipping tongs leave barely noticeable marks.

4 Once you've got a good grip, plunge the piece into the bucket of glaze. Hold it there for a moment, then lift it out, allowing the excess to flow off. Gently set the piece on a table covered with newspapers, and move on to the next one.

5 Any resulting bare spots can be healed later. Just dab on a bit of glaze with a brush or finger, then rub it smooth once it dries.

6 Stir the glaze bucket periodically throughout the glazing process, because the heavier materials in some glazes may settle quickly to the bottom.

Pouring

Less glaze is needed for the pouring technique. You'll need a wide bucket or basin to catch the runoff. The glaze should be about the same consistency as for dipping.

1 Starting with the interior of your form, pour in the glaze and swill it around as you pour it back out. Sounds simple enough, but there are a couple of pitfalls to avoid.

2 If you begin pouring the glaze out too soon, you'll run out before the whole interior is covered. And you want to work quickly, to prevent the form from absorbing too thick a layer of glaze on the bottom.

3 The trick is to fill the form with glaze at least a third of the way up the wall. Then immediately hold the form over the basin, at a low angle that brings the glaze up to the brink of the lip but doesn't allow it to spill over just yet.

4 In the same motion, begin to rotate the form. When you've covered about half the interior, you can begin to slowly dispel glaze, as you continue your rotation until all is glazed.

5 Dry practice your grasp to make sure you're in the proper position to complete the rotation in one fell swoop. Shake off the last few drips and the inside is done.

6 Ceramists often pour the interior and dip the exterior, if they have sufficient glaze mixed up. If you don't, pour away. Place the ware upside down on a wire rack set over a wide, empty basin or glaze bucket. (You can use a cooling rack or a shelf from an old refrigerator or stove.)

7 Pour glaze over the form until all areas are covered. Leave it to dry in place until it's dry enough to handle. Alternatively, you can hold the ware with glaze-dipping tongs while pouring glaze over it. Then you'll be able to set one piece down and move on to the next.

8 Pouring can also serve as a sophisticated decorative technique, with different colors of glaze poured into overlapping patterns.

However you get the glaze onto the ware, check the glaze thickness after the first coat has dried. Use a needle tool to make a scratch in the surface of the dry glaze, right through to the clay. Experience and familiarity with the characteristics of different glazes will tell you when the coat is just right, but a general rule is that it should be about the thickness of a thin coin. You may need an additional coat or two for proper results.

Applying Wax Resist

You must make sure glaze doesn't cover the bottom of your ware, or the piece will become a permanent fixture on your glaze shelf when the glaze melts and fuses to it.

To prevent this, apply a layer of wax resist all along the bottom and a slight bit up the sides. How far up depends upon whether you're using a runny glaze (wax a bit higher for more fluid glazes; no need to worry with stiffer ones). The resist helps keep the glaze from melting onto the kiln shelf. And it can add some personality to the piece to show a bit of clay at the bottom

Don't use your best brush to apply wax, because it could get ruined without proper care. Rub some dishwashing liquid into the hairs before dipping it into the wax; the soap forms a protective barrier that helps repel the wax. Keep soapy water on hand while you work; immediately after you're done, wash the brush with more soap and water.

Wax resist repels glaze adhesion and can be used for decorative purposes, as well as for protecting the bottom of forms.

Working with the Clay Itself

Of all the stages at which you can decorate a ceramic surface, you're most at one with your form at the wet to leather-hard stage, when the memory of creating it is fresh in your mind and on your hands. It's a great time to start the decorating process. The experience can be exhilarating, and the results can be spectacular.

Place a hand on the inside of the form to support the wall while applying decoration to the outside.

THE EARLIER YOU START THINKING about and working with the decorative surface, the more integrated the decoration will be to the form. And at this early stage, you can add depth and textural interest with techniques that can only be used at this stage.

This chapter offers an array of tantalizing techniques for wet to leather-hard clay, techniques that take full advantage of clay's malleable

HELPFUL TO REVIEW

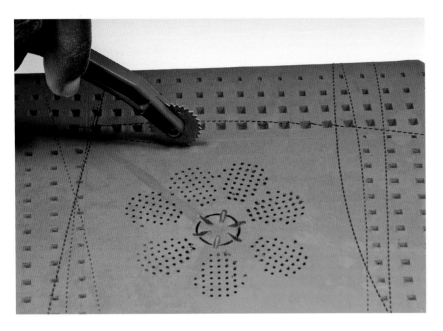

quality. You can press things into it (impressing, stamping, paddling); build on it (appliqué); cut into it (incising); and fill the cut-out lines with colored clay (inlay).

All these techniques will help you achieve a oneness with the clay itself. The clay will still be pliable, so you'll need to be sensitive to its condition to avoid distorting or destroying your form as you decorate it. Decorating your ware when it's too wet could collapse it; if it's too dry, you could crack it. With a bit of experience, you'll quickly learn to time it perfectly.

And if you're working with a vertical piece, remember to give it some extra support. As you decorate the outside, support the inside with your other hand.

Rouletting, stamping, carving away, and attaching additional pieces of clay are among the decorative techniques available at the wet-to leatherhard stage of clay work.

Impressing

FOR WET CLAY

Impressing takes full advantage of wet clay's most distinctive characteristics: its softness, malleability, and eagerness to accept any mark you might want to push into it. This wet ware technique involves pressing pliable textured items into the clay's surface, usually with your fingers or a small roller.

▼ **Tools**

Pony roller, rolling pin

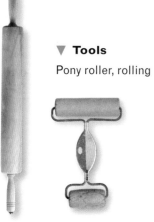

All sorts of objects are suitable for impressing into clay. Explore and experiment. Search for textured, flexible materials and objects around the house, the ground outside, in hardware stores, even at yard sales. String, wire, chains, lacy trim and textured fabrics, netting and mesh, strongly veined leaves—all are good candidates. **1**

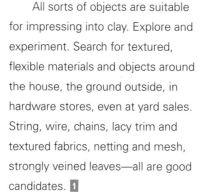

Before you begin, check the softness and wetness of the clay. If it's too firm, you'll have to use a great deal of pressure. You could severely distort your piece and still not end up with a good impression.

Position your textured object where you want it on the surface of your piece. Then, with firm, even pressure, use your fingers or the pony roller to press it into the clay. When you're sure the object has been sufficiently embedded, carefully pull it up to reveal its freshly made mark in the clay. **2**

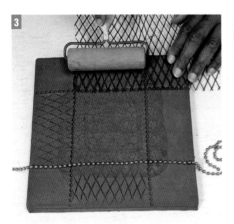

■ DESIGN CONSIDERATIONS

The doily provided the central floral element called for in my design directive. The blank space around it did create a border of sorts, but the soft impression from the doily was too close in value to the blank border to give me the variety, contrast, and emphasis I was striving for. So I used a ball chain to create some bold linear elements that helped clearly define the border. Then I created a midtone value in the border by pressing a piece of mesh into the rectangular spaces. **3**

   After all that, the four corners were calling out for attention, so I made spiral motifs by curling up a smaller ball chain. This provided a bit of unity by repeating the dotted line motif of the larger ball chain—as do the spiral shapes themselves, which echo the curlicues in the doily. As you can see, overlapping textures are not only allowed, but they can also produce very interesting effects.

■ FINISHING SUGGESTIONS

With any wet ware or leather-hard technique that creates a textured surface, you'll want a finish that emphasizes the texture. Staining is an excellent choice. Alternatively, there are glazes whose color varies with the thickness of their application. Because the glaze will be thicker in the recesses and thinner on the high points, the texture will be enhanced. If you make your test tiles with incised grooves (see page 46), you'll know which of your glazes act this way.

A stain highlights the texture of this impressed tile.

■ TEXTURE MATS

Texture mats make it a breeze to impress large areas of designed or simulated texture. Several designs and varieties are available commercially.

   Start with a fresh slab rolled to your desired size. Place the mat, textured side down, on your slab, and roll over it with a rolling pin. Before pulling the mat off entirely, take a peek to make sure the pattern has been satisfactorily embedded into the clay. **4**

   You can easily make your own texture mat from a sheet of craft foam. Just cut out the shapes you want with scissors, or use precut shapes—perfect for repeat patterns. Arrange the shapes on a base sheet of foam (a full-size sheet, or just a strip for decorative edges or borders). Glue them down with craft glue, and allow to dry. **5**

▶ **Tip:** If you're working on a three-dimensional object, decorate the slab first, while it's still flat on the table, then use it to form your piece.

Stamping
FOR WET CLAY

While impressing involves pressing a pliable object into the clay, stamping—and its mobile variant, rouletting—involves pressing or rolling the wet clay surface with a hard, rigid object.

▼ **Tools**

Stamps

JUST ABOUT ANY HARD, TEXTURED OBJECT HAS POTENTIAL.
Time to hit the flea markets and knickknack drawer once again. The world is your toolbox! Roll out a test slab and see what works—and what doesn't.

To stamp, just grasp your chosen object, press it firmly into the wet clay, and lift it straight up, so as not to distort your freshly stamped image. **1**

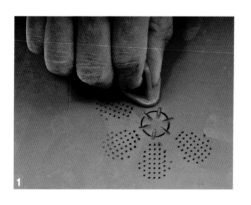

1

RELATED TECHNIQUES

Impressing	Staining	Glazing
36	**92**	**96**

■ MAKING STAMPS

If your found objects don't quite satisfy, you can always make your own stamps from bisqued clay. Using a fine-grain clay, first roll out a short, thick coil that flares out on one end—sort of like a fat, stubby mushroom stem. Tap the wide end on a piece of canvas to flatten and flare it a bit further. This is your *plug*. **2**

There are two ways to create the stamping surface. The fastest and easiest is to mold it around an object, such as a button or a small shell. Spray your object with some kind of releasing agent, such as a cooking or lubricating spray, and press it firmly, but not too deeply, into the wide, flat end of your plug. Remove the object carefully, so as not to distort the image, and allow your plug to firm up to leather hard. **3** At that stage you can make any necessary refinements, using a pointed modeling tool or a needle tool.

A second option is to carve your own image into the stamp. Allow the plug to firm up to leather hard. Then use a carving tool, a pointed modeling tool, or even a pencil to carve out your design. **4**

After your stamps have dried completely, bisque fire them, and they're ready to use.

> ▶ **Tip:** Keep in mind that the image on your stamp will be reversed in the clay—the raised areas on the stamp will be recessed in the clay, and the recessed areas on the stamp will be raised on the clay. If you plan to make a letter stamp, remember that the letters will be backward; carve accordingly. The stamped image will also be smaller, because of the shrinkage of the clay.

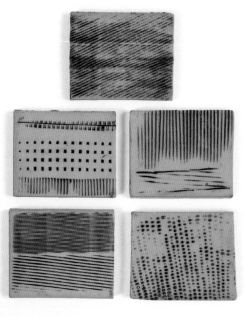

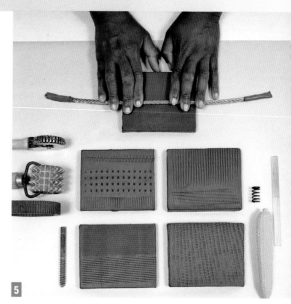

■ ROULETTING

Rouletting consists of rolling a cylindrical or wheeled textured object across a wet clay surface. Once again there are a slew of reappropriated items that could fill the bill.

▼ Tools
Roulettes

Roulette decoration is beautifully accented when stain is applied after the bisque, then glaze fired.

Pencil sharpener gears, springs, piecrust crimpers, rolling meat tenderizers—all are good prospects. Even a golf ball can be rolled across the clay's surface to make an interesting pattern. **5**

■ DESIGN CONSIDERATIONS

Once I had stamped my central floral image, I decided to frame it by using a rolling meat tenderizer to roulette the border. **6** The design needed some movement and a bit of playfulness; a dressmaker's tracing wheel, borrowed from my sewing kit, provided just the fluid lines I was looking for. **7**

■ FINISHING SUGGESTIONS

As with impressed decoration, choose a finish that emphasizes the texture—a stain, or glazes that vary in color with the thickness of their application. After first staining the texture with copper carbonate, I chose a white matte glaze to cover, thus allowing the oxide to bleed through to the surface.

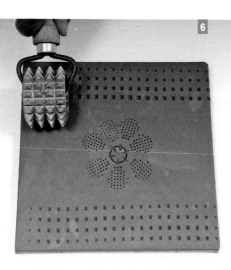

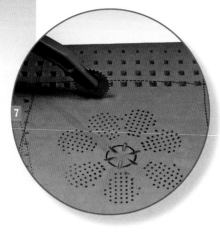

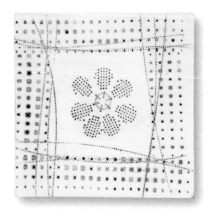

RELATED TECHNIQUES

Impressing	Staining	Glazing
36	**92**	**96**

Paddling

FOR LEATHER-HARD CLAY

Paddling is an effective way to create areas of texture on your work. It simply entails hitting the clay surface repeatedly with a rigid paddle—anything that has a handle on one end and a textured surface on the other—until a pleasing pattern emerges.

▶ **Tools**
Paddles

Paddles are available commercially, or you can roam about the house reappropriating likely items. The short-handled brush at top right in photo 1 was minding its own business in the garage until I gave it a new purpose in life. It's also easy enough to make your own from component parts. **1**

To create a good overall texture, you'll need to control the force, placement, and frequency of your strikes. Practice on some test pieces of clay to get a feel for what your paddles can do. My short-handled brush made a great texture in a few quick hits. Paddles with more subtle textures may require many repeated strikes to develop a satisfactory surface.

2

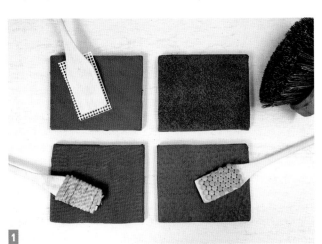

1

■ FINISHING SUGGESTIONS

Paddled textures can be finished by staining with a dark underglaze, as shown in photo 2, or by following any of the other suggestions offered in Impressing (see page 36). **2**

RELATED TECHNIQUES

Staining

■ MAKING PADDLES

Wooden kitchen utensils, Ping-Pong paddles, and scrap pieces of wood all make serviceable bases. If you use scrap plywood or planks, cut out a comfortable handle with a jigsaw and sand down the rough edges.

Then the hunt is on for materials that can be glued to the surface to create interesting textures. Cord and rope are good choices. Small components glued in formation, like the woodworking pegs shown in the photo at bottom right, work well, as does a piece of a textured material, such as the cross-stitch netting at top left. A Ping-Pong paddle already has a texture on one side, but if you're especially fond of its ready-made handle, you can remove the coating on the other side and add a different texture, for two paddles in one.

Alternatively, you can texture the wood surface itself by slashing a pattern into it with a saw blade or drilling a series of holes.

▶ **Tip:** Wood glue works well when adhering porous materials to wooden handles, but nonporous materials, such as plastic, will need an appropriately rated adhesive.

Wooden kitchen utensils were transformed into paddles by (left to right) gluing on a piece of cross-stitch mesh; slashing lines with a saw blade; wrapping and gluing cord (as shown), then adhering burlap; and gluing on rows of small wooden pegs.

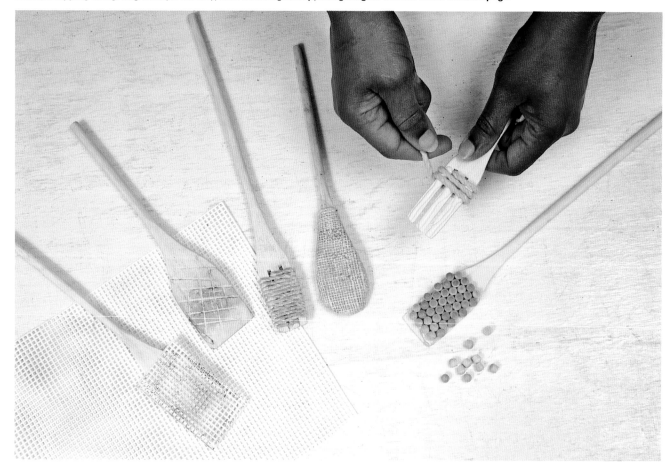

RELATED TECHNIQUES

Staining

Clay Appliqué

FOR WET TO LEATHER-HARD CLAY

You can add wonderful dimensionality and visual power to your work with clay appliqué—adhering pieces of moist clay to the leather-hard surface of a piece. Appliqués can be cut from a slab, shaped by hand, or formed in a mold.

▶ **Tools**
Rubber-tipped modeling tool, needle tool, metal scoring tool

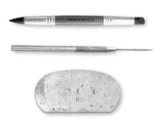

▶ **Video Tip:** To watch a video of me making and applying a clay appliqué, visit www.larkbooks.com/crafts

■ MAKING APPLIQUÉS

Raised appliqués that are flat and uniform in thickness can be cut from thin slabs of clay, using a needle tool. If you want multiples of the same shape for a repeat pattern, a cookie cutter can make quick work of it. **1**

Appliqués can also be shaped by hand, which works best for highly three-dimensional and organic forms. Depending on the shape you have in mind, start with a small ball or coil of clay. As you work out the general dimensions, be sure to flatten the bottom for attachment purposes, by tapping it on your worktable a few times. **2**

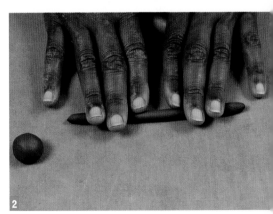

Sprigs make great appliqués, especially when you want repeated relief shapes. Dimensional on the front and flat on the back, sprigs are molded in a sprig mold (which is any mold you use to make a sprig). Simply press moist clay firmly into your mold, making sure it's completely filled and that all your detail is picked up by the clay. **3**

Use a knife to cut off the excess clay evenly, to create a flat base for attachment. And while you're at it, score the bottom of your sprig while it's still in the mold. **4**

To remove the sprig from the mold, take a pinch of fresh clay and press it gently into the sprig. They should grab each other just enough to let you pull the sprig straight out. **5**

Detach your temporary "handle" and lay the sprig out on your worktable, where you can straighten and trim it, if necessary.

■ ATTACHING APPLIQUÉS

The ideal time to attach appliqués is when the piece is still somewhat wet, just barely leather hard.

To begin, score both the back of the appliqué and the contact area on the piece. A metal rib works well on a good-size appliqué. **6** In cramped quarters, a needle tool works nicely. **7** Brush both scored surfaces with a good layer of slip to ensure a good bond. **8**

Press the two slipped surfaces firmly together, working over the whole

appliqué from the center outward, to make sure that the surfaces are in full contact and there are no air pockets trapped between them. If a little slip oozes out, let it firm up ever so slightly, then use a rubber-tipped modeling tool to smooth out the seam. Check for and compress any gaps, filling with a tiny coil of fresh clay if necessary. **9**

Keep in mind that techniques can be combined effectively. Stamping these flat appliqués made them more dimensional, and much more interesting.

■ FINISHING SUGGESTIONS

Some clay appliqués are smooth, others highly textured. Textured surfaces would benefit from the finishes suggested in the Impressing section (see page 36), while smoother surfaces could successfully receive just about any slip, underglaze, or glaze decorating technique described in the following chapters. On this particular tile, I utilized three different glazes that pooled and changed colors in the deeper recesses of the textured areas.

■ MAKING SPRIG MOLDS

Plaster sprig molds are available in a broad variety of forms, including alphabets, numerals, and images of all sorts. If you don't find what you want, it's easy to make them yourself out of clay.

A sprig mold is basically a beefed-up stamp mold, made in a similar way. (See "Making Stamps," page 39.) But for a sprig mold, you'll need a bigger and wider plug.

To make a mold using an interesting object—the easiest way to do it—spray it with a lubricant and press it into the flat end of the plug, deep enough to develop walls that will contain and shape the clay that you will pack into it. **10** Carefully remove the object—I'm using a button here—and you have a mold. **11**

After the mold firms up to leather hard, you can add details or definition, if needed, with a modeling or needle tool. Allow the mold to dry, then bisque fire it.

Incising

FOR WET TO LEATHER-HARD CLAY

▼ **Tools**
Incising tools, ribbon carving tools, wire loop tools

▼ **Tools**
Incising tools, ribbon carving tools, wire loop tools

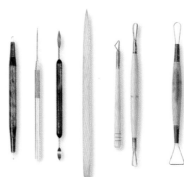

Incising is the removal of clay by cutting into the surface with a tool, thus leaving a distinctive mark. These incised marks can take the form of simple carved lines, repeated gestures that create interesting patterns or textures, or a carefully sculpted relief image.

THERE ARE A MULTITUDE OF TOOLS that can be used to cut into the surface of the clay, as well as a multitude of ways to manipulate them to create different marks. So it pays to experiment to find the tool, the action, and the clay stage that best suits your goals.

For example, wire loop tools can slice cleanly through a smooth-textured clay, but groggier clays seem to work better with ribbon carving tools that have a sharpened edge. I've found that gestural incisions work just fine in a softer, wetter clay, but for clear, crisp carvings, you should work on a leather-hard piece. **1**

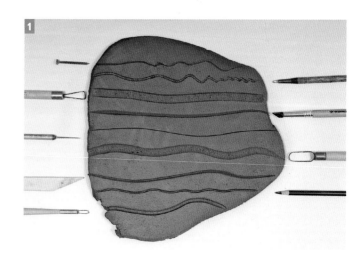

RELATED TECHNIQUES

Staining   Glazing
92   **96**

■ CREATING TEXTURE

The tool you use, along with the direction, angle, intensity, and frequency of your incised strokes, will affect the texture you produce. Select a few tools to try out, and see how many interesting textures you can come up with.

As you experiment, you'll learn how much clay you need to remove to create various textures, which will help you determine how thick you should make your pieces. A good starting point is to make the walls twice as thick as usual, but more vigorous decoration might require even thicker walls. **2**

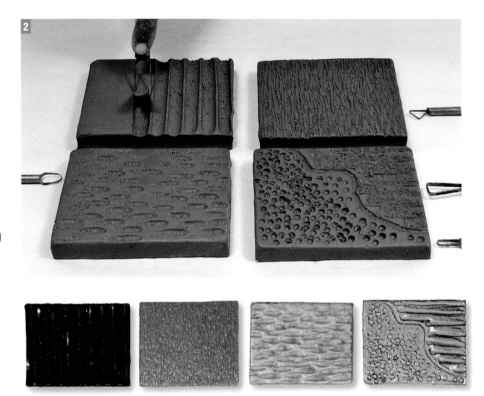

A variety of texture-accentuating glazes were used to glaze these four incised tiles.

■ CARVING A DESIGN

If you're carving a design or a relief image, it's a good idea to sketch your design on the piece in pencil before you cut. Alternatively, you can use transfer techniques to lay in some guidelines. (See "Transferring to Wet or Leather-hard Clay," page 29.) An incising tool that comes to a bit of a point works beautifully here to carve the lines of this simple line drawing. **3**

Relief images can be developed through further carving. Digging slightly deeper right next to the subject in your image makes the subject appear to protrude from the picture plane, creating an illusion of depth. **4**

▶ **Video Tip:** To watch a video of me carving and incising a tile, visit www.larkbooks.com/crafts.

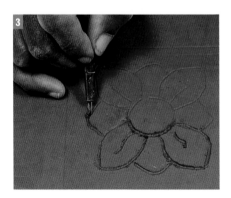

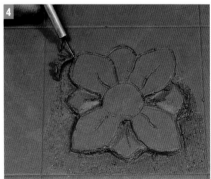

In relief work, it's critical that you remain conscious of the thickness of your walls, so that you don't create weak spots by removing too much clay, or removing it unevenly. If you're worried, probe several spots with a needle tool to check for thickness. **5** You can patch weak spots by scoring, applying slip, and compressing moist clay onto the spot. Allow it to firm up to leather hard before recarving it.

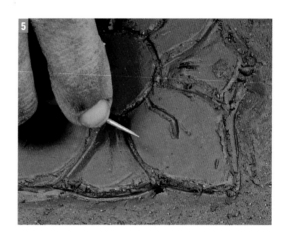

■ FINISHING SUGGESTIONS

Follow the finishing recommendations for impressed decoration on page 37, using stains and glazes that will emphasize the texture you've created. For the tile shown here, I used a turquoise glaze that pooled to a darker color in the dips and crevices of my carved decoration.

■ DESIGN CONSIDERATIONS

To balance the big, chunky flower in the center of this tile, I needed a bold treatment for the border. Using a wide, wire loop carving tool, I carved parallel furrows along the edge. This pattern of carving is called *fluting*, because it is reminiscent of the flutes, or grooves, in a classical column. **6**

RELATED TECHNIQUES

Staining   Glazing
92   **96**

Inlaid Colored Clay

FOR WET CLAY

Inlaying colored clay adds color and shape early on in the creation of your piece. The process is reminiscent of working with colored paper collages in that you start out by laying down your big background shapes, then add your smaller shapes on top. The major difference is you'll be cutting your shapes out of thin slabs of colored clay instead of paper (and you won't be making a big fat mess with glue).

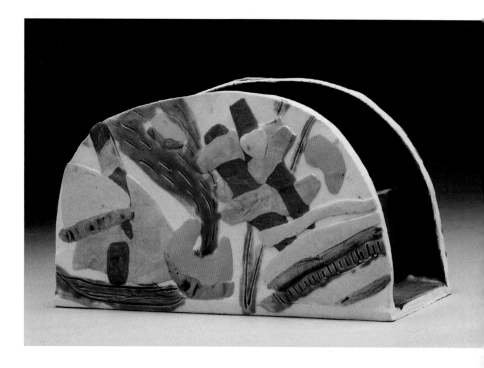

▼ **Tools**

Rolling pin, pony roller, needle tool, incising tool, cookie cutter, sgraffito loop tool

BEFORE YOU DO ANYTHING ELSE, plan your design, especially your colors; you'll want all of your colored clay shapes ready to use when you start the inlay. Roll wafer-thin slabs of each color between two sheets of wax paper. The wax paper keeps the slabs moist and prevents them from sticking to your roller.

Now roll out a fresh slab of your clay body. This will be your working slab, the base upon which you build your image. It's also the slab with which you can continue building once you are done with the inlay, so be sure to roll it out in the shape you'll need for the form you plan to make.

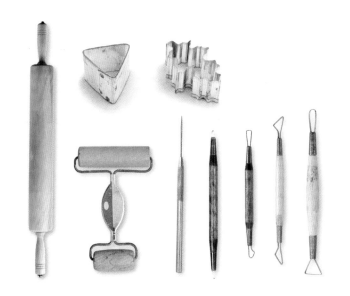

RELATED TECHNIQUES

Incising   Underglazes
46   **75**

You're ready to decorate. Cut out your shapes, using a needle tool or cookie cutter. Overlapping shapes can be sandwiched together before arranging them on your base slab. **1**

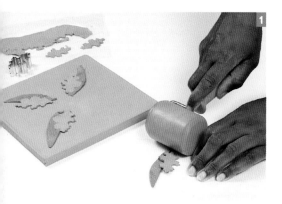

When your arrangement is complete, lay a sheet of wax paper over your work, and use a rolling pin or pony roller to level out your design. Because the clay will stretch, you're bound to get a bit of distortion, so keep an eye on the direction and the pressure you exert, to either minimize or exaggerate that distortion to your advantage. The thinner your colored slabs, the less pressure required, and the less distortion you'll get. **2**

■ DESIGN CONSIDERATIONS

With my central floral image established, it was time to work on the border. The predominantly warm-toned center was calling out for some cool tones. Thin strips of blue clay addressed that aesthetic concern. The repetition of lines in the crenulated edge also added rhythm and movement to the composition. **3**

Looking it over, I decided a bit of texture would add variety to the surface, so I incised a few lines into the leaves. **4** Actually, any of the other techniques in this chapter can be combined with inlaid colored clay.

■ FINISHING SUGGESTIONS

A clear glaze accentuates and brightens the pure colors of inlaid clays, but interesting effects can also be achieved with lightly tinted transparent glazes. Another good option is to leave the work unglazed altogether, for a softer, subtler look. For this tile, I applied two lightly tinted transparent glazes: a pale, straw-colored glaze in the center, and a pale, baby blue one on the border.

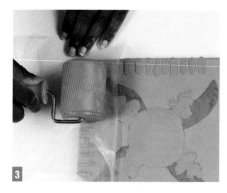

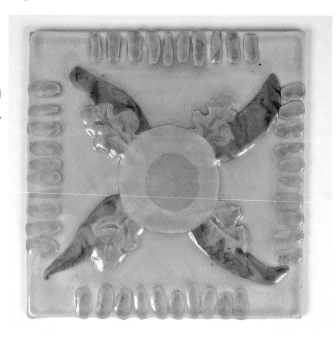

■ MAKING COLORED CLAY

Clay is generally colored by mixing ⅓ to 1 ounce (10–30 ml) of stain or coloring oxide into each pound (0.45 kg) of clay, depending on the intensity desired. You can add color to any clay, but the cleanest, brightest colors start with white or lightly colored clay. As always, test and experiment.

If you don't have access to a scale, or would rather not deal with powdered stains and oxides, you can use an intensely colored underglaze instead. It needs to dry and thicken a bit, ideally to the consistency of paste. You might try leaving the jar open for a few days or pouring some underglaze into a shallow bowl to increase evaporation. Or you can search through your older colors and find a perfect candidate that is drying up on its own.

For each ½ pound (226.8 g) of clay, you'll need 1 to 2 ounces (30–60 ml) of underglaze—between a half and a whole small jar. But test your own materials to make sure. A ½ pound of colored clay goes a long way for inlay, so you may want to make less if you're trying this on just a piece or two.

When the underglaze is the proper consistency, roll out your weighed clay, don a pair of rubber gloves, and spread the underglaze on the surface. 5 If necessary, allow it to sit out and firm up more, especially if the underglaze was on the wet side. When it's firm enough, roll up the slab like a jelly roll. 6 Then work the color in by squeezing and kneading the clay with your hands. 7 When the color is uniformly worked into the clay, wrap it in plastic wrap or put it in a plastic bag, to keep it from drying out or contaminating other colors.

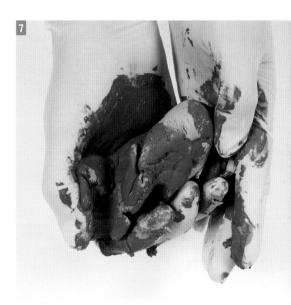

Gallery

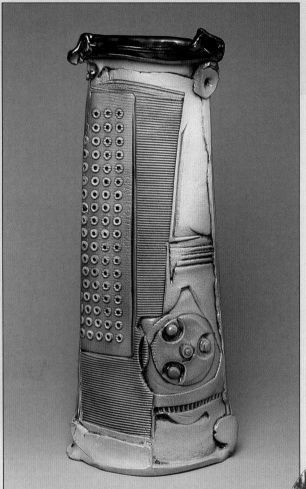

Silvie Granatelli
Green Teapot, 2009

8 x 7 x 5 inches (20.3 x 17.8 x 12.7 cm)
Wheel-thrown porcelain; hand carved at leather-
hard stage; gas fired, cone 10
Photo by Molly Selznick

Sandra Blain
Furrowed #2, 2009

23 x 9½ x 6½ inches (58.4 x 24.1 x 16.5 cm)
Slab-constructed red stoneware clay; brushed
and sprayed slip, found-object impressions,
oxides rubbed into textures on bisque piece;
multiple glazes sprayed; electric kiln; cone 6
oxidation
Photo by Michael Healy

Sarah Heimann
Tall Vase, 2009

9 x 4¾ x 3½ inches (22.9 x 12 x 8.9 cm)
Wheel-thrown and altered white stoneware;
carved, incised through slip and sigillata; bisque
cone 06; fake ash glaze brushed on and wiped
back; electric fired, cone 6
Photos by Glen Scheffer

Sandi Pierantozzi
Canister Set, 2006

Largest, 6 x 5 x 4 inches (15.2 x 12.7 x 10.2 cm)
Slab-built porcelain; impressed design; electric
fired, cone 6; satin glaze
Photo by artist

Jenny Lou Sherburne
Belted, Ruffled Vase, 2007

17 x 4 x 4 inches (43.2 x 10.2 x 10.2 cm)
Wheel-thrown, pinched, and stacked stoneware;
carved, stippled with appliqué, electric fired with
slip, cone 5; glazes, cone 5-6
Photo by Tom Mills

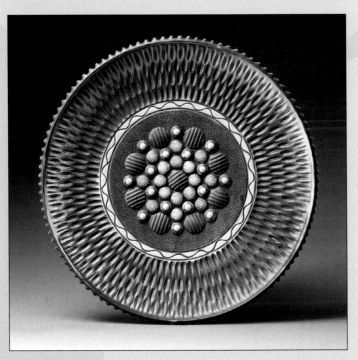

Amy Higgason
Wall Platter, 2008

14 x 14 x 1½ inches (35.6 x 35.6 x 3.8 cm)
Wheel-thrown white stoneware; carved with
attached clay sprigs; Josh Green matte glaze and
T13 green gloss glaze; electric fired, cone 6
Photo by Guy Nicol

Lynn Fisher
Tall Vases, 2008

Largest, 16 x 8½ x 6½ inches (40.6 x 21.6
x 16.5 cm); smallest, 12 x 6½ x 4¾ inches
(30.5 x 16.5 x 12 cm)
Hand-built porcelain; electric fired, cone 9
Photo by artist

Working with Slip

Slip—merely liquid clay, but oh, the possibilities it has to offer! This marvelous material can be substantial enough to provide semisculptural decoration, yet smooth and fluid enough to provide a beautiful, blemish-concealing base for other decorative techniques.

WE WILL EXPLORE THE GAMUT OF SLIP TECHNIQUES, starting with combing and chattering, techniques that take full advantage of slip's soft but substantial nature to create visual and physical texture. The former will have us playing with our fingers and combs; the latter, with our brushes.

If you've ever squeezed mustard onto a hot dog with flourish, or written "Happy Birthday" on a cake, then you've already executed the basic technique of slip trailing. You can even use mustard or ketchup squeeze bottles for slip, though smaller bottles, available from ceramic supply houses, provide better control.

With sgraffito, we'll reach for our incising tools (see page 22) and scratch our design through a layer of slip, exposing the color of the clay below.

Inlaid slip decoration combines a few familiar decorative techniques to take us in a totally new direction. Carved trenches are filled with slip, creating a design that is inlaid to the surface of the ware.

As wonderful as slip may be, there may be places where you don't want it. Resists come to the rescue. We'll explore a few different resist options, including wax, paper, and found objects.

Finally, we'll work with a velvety smooth version of slip called terra sigillata. Made from the finest of clay particles, "terra sig" has special properties that enable it to achieve a glossy, sensuous surface unique among slips.

Combing with Underglaze and Oxides

FOR WET TO LEATHER-HARD CLAY

Running your fingers or tools through freshly laid slip to create a decorative line or texture is called combing. The smooth, wet surface calls out to be touched—fingered, combed, or manipulated with a toothed tool to create a myriad of possible textures.

◀ **Tools**
Combing tools

DECORATIVE WET WARE SLIP should have the consistency of pancake batter—fluid, yet substantial. Start by applying a good thick coat to your clay—brushing, pouring, or dipping, as you prefer.

Using your fingers to manipulate slip into interesting gestural configurations harkens back to finger painting in primary school, a time when creative juices ran bold and free. It can be a fun and immediate way to decorate your piece. **1**

Interesting textures can also be obtained with a variety of wide-toothed combs. **2**

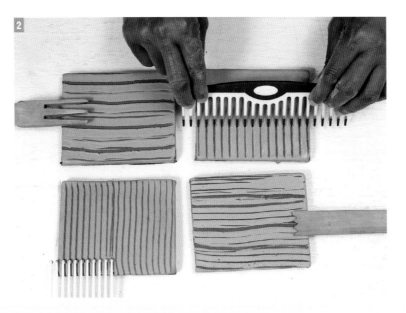

The allure of combing is its immediacy, the expressiveness of freezing a gestural moment in the slip. Hesitation strokes will not read well. So after experimenting a bit, visualize and practice what you would like to do before you begin your actual piece. Then apply the slip, take a deep breath, and set those fingers and combs to work. If (heavens!) you should make an errant mark, simply smooth it over, reapply the slip, and begin again.

Note the diverse character that these two distinct glazes give slip decoration. **D**epending on its tint and degree of transparency, the covering glaze can help maintain bold contrasts, as with the lightly tinted transparent glaze on the right, or imbue the slip decoration with subtle mystery, as with the glaze on the left.

■ FINISHING SUGGESTIONS

Textural slip decoration can be left unglazed or covered with a clear, transparent, translucent, or semiopaque glaze. Translucent and semiopaque glazes are most effective when used over slip decoration that boldly contrasts with the color of the clay body. To finish my sample tile, I applied a deep green translucent glaze.

■ DESIGN CONSIDERATIONS

The project tile illustrates the variety that combing can provide, depending on the tools you use. I wanted a bold center for the flower; my index finger produced it. **3** The petals needed somewhat finer lines; a rubber-tipped tool complied. **4** With just simple lines so far, the border cried out for variety and texture; a wide-toothed comb answered the call. **5**

Chattering

FOR WET TO LEATHER-HARD CLAY

When slip is brushed onto a surface, it's normally applied in smooth, flowing strokes with a soft, wide brush. Chattering is the exception. With this technique, the slip is brushed on in a disruptive manner, to create a repetitive pattern from the thick and thin variations of the brush strokes.

▼ **Tools**

Fan brush, flat house-painting brush

Previously I've stressed the need for soft-haired brushes, fully charged with material. Not so with chattering. Wide brushes with stiffer bristles tend to create more texture, and a drier brush delivers more uneven, and thus more textural, results. Fan brushes provide interesting effects as well. Experiment with a variety of different motions and an array of different brushes, to see how many different textures and patterns you can create. **1**

Deeply colored translucent glazes, like the one used here, tend to accentuate the unevenness of chattered slip decoration. The results can be textures of subtle beauty and great depth.

■ DESIGN CONSIDERATIONS

A fan brush can produce great textural effects. To make my central floral motif, I held the brush perpendicular to the surface, to create wispy, flyaway petals. **2**

Trimming a few bristles off a cheap house-painting brush increases its texture potential. I snipped a zigzag pattern into the tip of this one, then brushed a charmingly ragged border. **3**

■ FINISHING SUGGESTIONS

Like combed surfaces, chattered decoration looks good unglazed, or finished with a clear, transparent, translucent, or semiopaque glaze. Translucent and semiopaque glazes look best when used over slip decoration that boldly contrasts with the color of the clay.

On this tile, I accentuated the central flower with a dark, translucent glaze, allowing it to dominate the border, with its lighter, more transparent glaze.

RELATED TECHNIQUES

Glazing

Trailing with Slip

FOR WET TO LEATHER-HARD CLAY, GREENWARE, AND BISQUE WARE

Trailing is the process of creating a decorative image or pattern by squeezing lines of slip or glaze from rubber or plastic bottles. As a bonus, slips (and a few glazes) retain their raised texture, thus adding dimension to your work.

▶ **Tools**

Trailing bottles

SLIP FOR TRAILING SHOULD BE THE CONSISTENCY OF PUDDING—thick, yet smooth. Just about any squeeze bottle will do as a trailer, but you'll have greater control with one of the specialized trailing bottles on the market. Fill your bottle, and you're almost ready to go.

Here's some insider info: Before putting your trailer to work, hold it with the point down and give a slight shake, to force out any air bubbles. Bubbles will make the trailer spit out a big splat in the middle of your nice line; you want to avoid that.

When you're ready, hold the tip of the bottle in the air slightly above the surface. Squeeze gently and allow the slip to be dispensed smoothly, moving the bottle in pace with the flow. You'll be tempted to use the bottle like a pencil, dragging the tip across the surface of your piece. Refrain. You'll get more fluid results if you follow the technique I suggest.

Practice on paper first, creating lines and then images, until you become familiar with the amount of pressure and speed necessary to create controlled lines. **1**

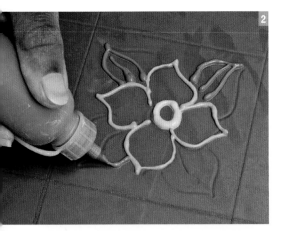

Slip trailing can make delightfully loose, expressive drawings on leather-hard clay. But when you're working with more precise imagery, having some guidelines to follow can be very helpful. (See "Transferring to Wet or Leather-hard Clay," page 29.) 2

DESIGN CONSIDERATIONS

With my central flower established, it was time to compose a frame. Yellow diagonal lines echoed the center of the flower, and they did imply a border. 3 But it all seemed ill defined. Outlining the blocks of yellow lines in blue slip provided the emphasis I wanted. 4

I could have stopped there, but the diagonal lines seemed to create a disjointed sense of movement. Cross-hatching the lines lent some stability and balance.

FINISHING SUGGESTIONS

If you've used a single color slip for your decoration, then the lines should show up through any clear, transparent, or translucent glaze, and some semiopaque ones, if the color of the slip contrasts sharply with the color of the clay body. Under an opaque glaze, the lines won't be visible to the eye, but they'll still be discernable to the touch, thus creating a subtle tactile texture, which could be interesting. A multicolor decoration such as I have used here works best under a clear or barely tinted transparent glaze, or when the piece is left unglazed. The tile shown is clear glazed.

Sgraffito with Slip

FOR WET TO LEATHER-HARD CLAY,
GREENWARE, AND BISQUE WARE

Sgraffito, which is pronounced "zgra-FEE-toe," derives from the Italian word *sgraffire*, meaning "to scratch." So it's no huge surprise that the technique refers to scratching (or carving) lines into a surface to reveal a different color clay or decorative material underneath.

▼ Tools

Ball stylus, loop stylus, needle tool, clean-up tool, bamboo modeling tool, ribbon carving tool, fettling knife

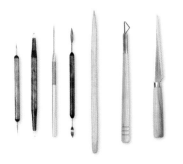

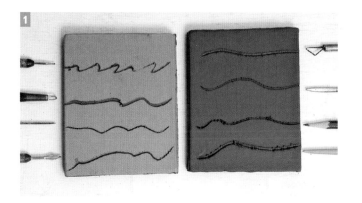

Sgraffito can be used with just about any combination of materials, at nearly all stages of clay work. It's most effective with highly contrasting colors. Here we explore its most common use: wet ware slip on leather-hard clay.

To get started, apply a good, solid, flowing coat of slip. Let the slip firm up until it too feels leather hard to the touch. As always, different tools will offer different results, thus expanding your visual vocabulary. Try out all your incising and carving tools. Varying sizes and qualities of lines will add diversity and interest to your composition. **1**

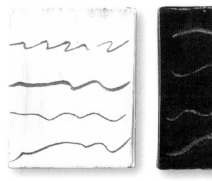

A clear glaze reveals the subtle differences in line quality between the various tools that were used to sgraffito these tiles.

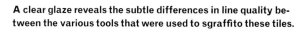

Freehand sgraffito strokes can be fun and expressive, but when you're working with a more exacting design, use the plastic-and-stylus method on page 29 to transfer the design to your piece. After the slip has firmed up to leather hard—it should look damp but feel dry to the touch—it's safe to lay your plastic transfer sheet down and impress your design lightly into the surface. Alternatively, you can sketch in the design lightly with a pencil.

Use a needle tool, an incising tool, or a specially designed sgraffito stylus to etch your image. As you carve lines through the slip, you'll create furrows that leave behind curled-up bits of excess slip. You'll want to brush those bits off right away, but don't do it just yet, or you'll smudge your image. **2**

▓ DESIGN CONSIDERATIONS

Because I was working with a multicolored design, I transferred my guidelines directly onto the bare, leather-hard tile, so I'd know where to paint the different colors of slip. That base color design gave me a structure to work within as I sgraffitoed the flower, lines, and leaves freehand.

To make sure that the central floral image was the focal point, I kept

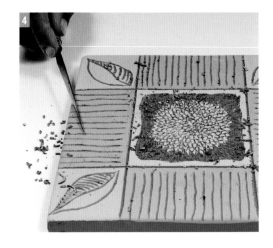

the border colors in cool tones, which are visually receding. That allowed the warm yellow to pop forward. To further emphasize the flower, I carved around it, creating some contrast between the light yellow and the dark red clay. Red clay sgraffito lines became the unifying element in the composition, knitting the cool border to the warm center. **3**

Once your piece has dried to the greenware stage, you can scrape off those little curls of dried slip with a knife blade. You'll definitely want to get them off before the bisque firing, when they will become too hard and sharp to remove easily. **4**

FINISHING SUGGESTIONS

If you've used slip in a single color—one that contrasts with the surface underneath—then the lines should show up through any clear, transparent, or translucent glaze, and some semiopaque ones. A multicolor decoration as I have used shows up best under a clear or barely tinted transparent glaze, or when the piece is left unglazed. This tile has a clear glaze.

Sgraffito as Accent

Effective as decorative and illustrative lines, sgraffito can also contribute accentuating lines for painterly, brushed decoration. A few deftly placed strokes can really bring a slip-painted image into sharp focus, as they did for this exuberant blue flower, painted in wet ware slip and vitreous underglazes.

Slip Inlay FOR WET TO LEATHER-HARD CLAY

Inlaid surfaces can be quite elegant. You create them by carving grooves into a leather-hard clay surface, filling the grooves with slip in a contrasting color, then scraping away the excess to reveal the inlaid image or pattern.

▶ **Tools**

Carving tool, trailing tool, metal rib, firm rubber rib

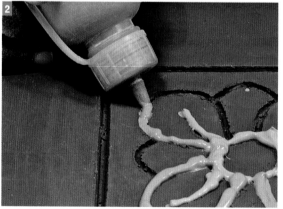

TO ESTABLISH YOUR DESIGN, use the leather-hard transfer method detailed on page 29, or sketch it in with a pencil or needle tool. With that done, etch your design into the surface with a carving tool. Be sure to carve a trench that is deep enough to hold a substantial amount of slip—at least ⅛ inch (3 mm) deep. If the trench is too shallow, you risk scraping away part of your design later. **1**

Now fill the incised lines with slip. Conventionally, the slip is brushed into the carved grooves, piled on thickly until it overflows the trench. Often several coats are required. A quicker way is to apply the slip directly into the grooves with a slip-trailing tool. Either way, keep checking as the slip dries and settles in. Reapply in any spots where the slip dips below the surface. **2**

RELATED TECHNIQUES

Incising	Glazing	Brushwork with Underglaze
46	**96**	**75**

■ FINISHING SUGGESTIONS

For single-color designs, any clear, transparent, or translucent glaze will serve. Multicolored designs fare better under a clear glaze or barely tinted transparent glaze, or when the piece is left unglazed. The tile shown is clear glazed.

After the slip has firmed up to soft leather hard, compress it into the grooves, using a firm rubber rib. With a complex multicolor design such as I have here, you can use a rubber-tipped tool to compress your lines one color at time, cleaning the tool after each color. **3**

When the slip is dry, scrape off the excess, either with a metal rib, for smooth- textured clays, or with a firm rubber rib, for groggier clays. Scrape in the direction of your line, rather than across it. In multicolor compositions, work one color at a time to avoid cross-contamination. **4**

Resists for Slip Decoration

Resists can take many forms, but they all do one basic job. They form a barrier between layers of decorative materials, or between decorative materials and the clay surface. As such, they can be used to create imagery, as well as protect it. Although the resist techniques below can be used or adapted for every stage of clay work, we'll focus on wet ware slip and leather-hard clay.

FOR WET TO LEATHER-HARD CLAY, GREENWARE, AND BISQUE WARE

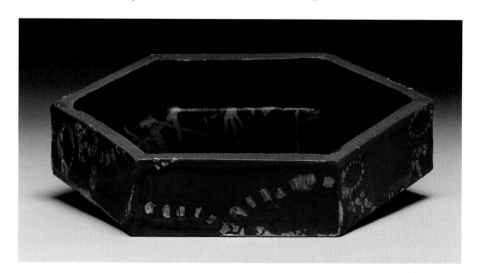

▲ **Tools and Materials**

Wax resist, brushes, scissors

▶ **Video Tip:** To watch a video of me using a resist as I do slip decoration, visit www.larkbooks.com/crafts.

■ **FOUND OBJECTS**

Used as resists, objects with interesting profiles or open weaves create intriguing silhouettes or textures. Plant material and fabrics offer some of the best potential.

Arrange your objects on a leather-hard surface, getting them to lie as flat as possible. Stubborn ones may have to be impressed slightly into the clay to make them stay put. Brush on a good flowing, even layer of slip, being careful not to let it pool in any spots. **1**

For the cleanest image, leave the resists in place until the slip has firmed up, then remove them to expose your image. If an object is hard to get hold of, use a needle tool to gently pry up an edge, then lift it off. **2**

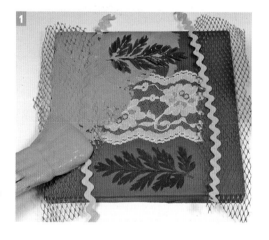

RELATED TECHNIQUES

Sgrafitto

A bit of lace, a couple of leaves, and some strips of rickrack worked together to create a circular motion. Along with some mesh from a bag of tangerines, they all served as resists beneath a layer of white slip. After the bisque firing, the tile was covered with an olive-tinted transparent glaze and refired.

The translucent orange glaze I applied after the bisque turned milky where it pooled in the grooves of the sgraffito, making the central flower a bit too delicate to compete with the bold frame. This would be a good candidate for post-firing techniques. (See page 110.)

■ PAPER

Lightweight paper or newsprint makes an excellent resist. Cut or tear your paper stencils, and arrange them in a pattern that pleases you. Lightly misting the surface of your piece with water will help them stick.

Gently spread and smooth them down, first with your fingers, then with a damp sponge, to work out any wrinkles. Brush on a good, flowing coat of slip, being careful not to dislodge the paper in the process. **3** Allow the slip to firm up before attempting to remove the resists. If any of them got a bit buried in slip, look for a slightly raised edge and resort to your needle tool again to coax it up, then peel it away and expose your pattern. **4**

WAX

Because wax resist is brushed on as a liquid, it can take on any intricate design that your brush can handle. It's most readily used at the glazing-on-bisque stage, but works wonderfully well with slip on leather-hard clay. (Directions for applying wax resist are on page 33.)

Sketch out your design with a needle tool, or transfer your image to the clay. Once the design is established, use a round brush with a good point for details, and a flat brush for large areas. By dipping your brush tip into a bit of dishwashing liquid first, you'll be able to use whichever brush in your collection suits the job, without fear of losing it to the wax. Be sure to let the wax dry before doing any more work on the piece. 5

To animate the border and add movement, I scratched a couple of sgraffito lines through the wax, exposing the clay and adding the energy of linear zigzag elements to the composition. 6

Once all the wax is dry, brush or pour a layer of slip onto the piece and allow it to firm up. Any excess that might have clung to a waxed area can be easily wiped off with a damp sponge. No need to remove the wax. It will burn off in the bisque firing. 7

FINISHING SUGGESTIONS

Resists can be used with any decorating material, at all stages of clay work. Follow the finishing suggestions for the specific decorating material you are using. With slip work, you may follow the finishing suggestions outlined for slip inlay on page 64.

The transparent amber glaze on this tile not only gave the slip a beautiful honeyed tone, but it also helped accentuate the strong contrast between the color of the slip and the color of the clay.

Terra Sigillata FOR GREENWARE AND BISQUE WARE

Terra sigillata is a unique breed of surface-decorating material—a slip that contains only the very finest particles of clay. Whereas regular slip would be dry and rough if left unglazed, "terra sig," when burnished, can acquire the sheen of a satin glaze, even a glossy one. Whether in natural clay colors or tinted with stains or oxides, terra sigillata surfaces have a soft, sensual appeal that begs to be touched.

▼ Tools

Brush, chamois, plastic wrap, burnishing stone, metal spoon

▶ **Tip:** Terra sigillata will continue to settle—that is, the heavier particles will continually sink to the bottom of the jar. Mix it thoroughly before you start, and stir or shake it frequently as you work.

TO MAKE TERRA SIGILLATA, clay and water are combined with a deflocculant, which suspends the finer clay particles as they separate from the heavier ones. After sitting for at least 24 hours, the mixture separates into three distinct layers: a layer of water at the top, a sludge of heavy clay particles on the bottom, and a suspension of fine clay particles in the middle—that's the terra sigillata. The water is siphoned off, as is the terra sig; both the water and the sludge are discarded. **1**

The color of terra sigillata depends on the color of the clay, so the predominant colors are earth tones (browns, reds, buff), grays, whites, and off-whites, but colorants can be added to the formula as well. Recipes and directions for mixing terra sigillata are found on page 123.

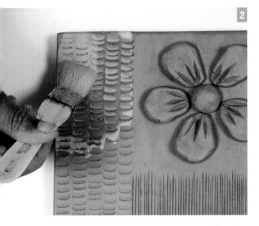

Apply terra sigillata to greenware or bisque ware with a soft-haired brush, using steady back and forth strokes, until you've accumulated an even and substantial layer. If fired at this point, the surface would be smooth but dry and stonelike. **2**

A good buffing with a piece of chamois or a thin piece of plastic will develop a light sheen. Working while the terra sig is slightly damp, start with a light touch and increase your pressure as the surface begins to gloss up. **3**

Bringing out an even shinier surface requires more elbow grease. Burnishing to a high gloss works best on rounded forms made of smooth clay with little or no grog to break free and scratch the surface while you work. Use a hard, smooth object, such as a rounded river stone or the back of a spoon, or stick with the chamois or plastic wrapped around your finger. **4**

The terra sigillatas on these salt and pepper shakers showed their true colors—white and rich black—when they were burnished and fired to temperature.

▓ LAYERING COLORS

When terra sigillata is applied to greenware, you can layer on additional colors of it after the bisque. This is especially effective on textured areas, but even smooth surfaces can develop a weathered, modulated look. Simply paint a contrasting color of terra sigillata onto the bisqued ware. When the surface still looks damp but is dry to the touch, use your plastic-covered finger to burnish firmly, which will begin to rub away the terra sig from the higher points of the surface, revealing bits of the bisqued color below. In photo **5** you can see the difference between the two tiles. Both tiles were coated at greenware stage with the same two colors of terra sig, and then fired once.

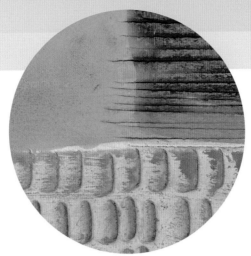

However, at that point, three additional colors of terra sig were rubbed into various areas of the tile on the right and then refired one more time. Note the extra emphasis this gives the texture and composition. **5**

■ FINISHING SUGGESTIONS

After buffing or burnishing the terra sigillata surface, all that's left to do is let it dry and fire the piece to bisque or maturing temperature, depending on what is to follow. This project tile was fired to maturing.

A popular alternative is to fire to a low bisque temperature, and then refire in a primitive pit or barrel firing, to mark the ware with the effects of the flame. Information on pit and barrel firing is on pages 120-121.

5

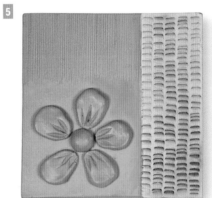

Slip Gallery

Ruchika Madan
Food Chain: Bird and Worms, 2009

9 x 6 x 1 inches (22.9 x 15.2 x 2.5 cm)
Slab-built and hump-molded white stoneware; slip decorated
with paper stencil and sgraffito, incised; gloss and matte
glazes; fired in cone 6 oxidation
Photos by artist

Kate Biderbost
Bowl, 2008

5 x 6 inches (12.7 x 15.2 cm)
Wheel-thrown white stoneware; slip brushwork;
glazed, soda fired, cone 10
Photo by William Biderbost

Laura Jean McLaughlin
Willow, 2008

16 x 10 x 6 inches (40.6 x 25.4 x 15.2 cm)
Hand-built porcelain; cone 6; slips, stains,
sgraffito
Photo by Dylan Vattone

Blaine M. Avery
Mess of Bowls, 2008

Each, 5½ x 5½ x 3½ (14 x 14 x 8.9 cm)
Wheel-thrown stoneware; slip trailing; porcelain slip under
translucent glaze; gas fired, cone 11; salt glazed
Photo by artist

Amy Higgason
Covered Jar, 2008

6 x 5¾ x 5¾ inches (15.2 x 14.6 x 14.6 cm)
Wheel-thrown white stoneware; sgraffito; brown and black
underglazes; electric fired, cone 6
Photo by Guy Nicol

Kathy King
Untitled, 2008

12 x 12 x 1 inches (30.5 x 30.5 x 2.5 cm)
Wheel-thrown porcelain; sgraffito carved; clear glaze;
oxidation fired, cone 6
Photos by artist

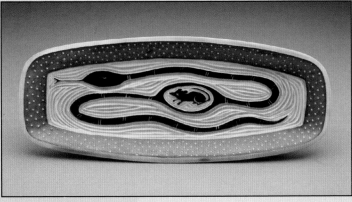

Ruchika Madan
Food Chain: Snake and Mouse, 2009

12 x 4½ x 2 inches (30.5 x 11.4 x 5.1 cm)
Slab-built and hump-molded white stoneware; sgraffito and
slip trailing; matte and gloss glazes; oxidation fired, cone 6
Photo by artist

Working with Underglazes, Stains, and Oxides

Underglazes are among the most versatile decorating materials. Available in a wide array of forms, from liquid to solid chalk, they can be applied with brush or with pen, by spray or by spatter. Stains and oxides, the coloring agents for underglazes, can also be used independently.

IN THIS CHAPTER WE BEGIN TO WORK WITH NOT ONLY NEW MATERIALS BUT ALSO WITH A NEW SURFACE: BISQUE. So far, we've worked on a more or less responsive clay surface; bisque is unyielding. Although we can no longer make marks in the clay, a rigid surface has its benefits.

If you've tried your hand at drawing and painting on paper, you'll find some familiar ground here. Underglazes let you mimic several works-on-paper techniques. If you've never made art on paper, fear not. You'll find all the information you need to play with clay.

Liquid underglaze brushwork can resemble tempera, but just water it down a bit, and soft, beautiful watercolor effects appear. Trailing tools with fine pen nibs combine with liquid underglaze to echo pen and ink washes. Ceramic chalk

and pencil are much firmer than their pastel counterparts, but they can still deliver a soft chalk effect, thanks to the bisque's abrasiveness. And aided by masks and stencils, we'll sponge, spatter, and spray the bisque surface.

All these techniques work best on smoother surfaces, so what about all that wonderful textural work you've learned to do? That's where staining comes in, darkening the deepest recesses of your surface and bringing your textural work into dramatic focus.

Because underglaze colors are truest on a white surface, I applied a white wet ware slip to the sample tiles in this chapter before bisque firing them. Staining is the exception; on those tiles, the color of the clay was left to interact with the stain.

HELPFUL TO REVIEW

Brushwork with Underglaze and Oxides

FOR GREENWARE AND BISQUE WARE

Like the brushes that create it, brushwork encompasses a broad variety of techniques and approaches. In this section we'll cover loose, impressionistic watercolor techniques and well-defined naturalistic painting, using liquid underglazes, with a brief nod to oxides.

▼ **Tools**

Brushes, watercolor palette

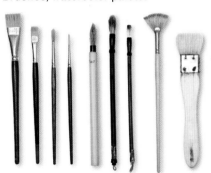

▓ BRUSHES

Different brushes produce different effects, from the calligraphic line of the Oriental brush to the super-thin line of the finest liner brush. Soft-haired brushes work best for even, fluid applications. Soft synthetics work incredibly well with underglaze. On the other hand, stiffer bristled brushes can create interesting texture (see "Chattering," for example, page 57). Play around with various brushes to see what kinds of marks you can make. Handling will be quite different from brushing with slip. ■

Once dry, my brushwork doodles were coated with a clear glaze and then fired.

RELATED TECHNIQUES

Chattering

WASHES

A wash is just a watered-down underglaze, but show some respect. Washes can give you a variety of tonal ranges from just one jar of underglaze, and make you feel like you just came home from the ceramic shop with a bagful of new underglaze colors.

To make a wash, put a small amount of water in a cup or small dish. Slowly add your underglaze until you've reached the intensity of color that you want. Test your washes on a white sheet of paper or, better yet, on a piece of scrap bisque. Make a range of tones by adding different amounts of color to separate batches of water. **2**

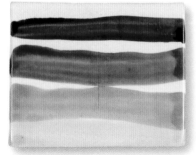

A coat of clear glaze and a firing highlight the variations in tone and color you can achieve by simply diluting underglazes with water.

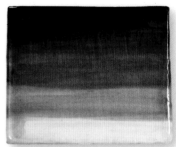

Gradients can establish a background for an image, because they help create a sense of depth.

If you run out of a tint as you paint, just mix some more and work the edge where you pick up again to make a smooth transition. Note: Work washes only on bisqued surfaces, because the blending and generous use of water will soften and wear away the clay surface of a green piece.

BLENDING A COLOR GRADIENT

There may be times when you need a gradient of dark to light—for a sky, perhaps, or a shadow. Mix your color right on the bisque surface. Starting in the area of your darkest tone, brush the full strength of the color about a third of the way down the section. Dip your brush into water and shake off the excess. Starting at about the middle of the full-strength area, blend the water and color together, working down the section. Continue dipping and spreading the color until you reach the end. You'll notice a gradual lightening as you keep adding water to the gradient.

If the results are not perfectly blended, rejoice that the bisque surface is forgiving. Simply return to the areas that need attention, and work in additional water to lighten or additional color to darken. **3**

WATERCOLOR TECHNIQUES

With these two basic blending techniques mastered, you're equipped to try watercolor techniques directly on bisque.

Start with your lightest colors and with your background areas, as I've done here, with a gradient of yellow for the wall and a wash of a mustard color for the tabletop. As I paint and add shading to the blue pot, I simply work compatible colors together while the surface is still wet, to create beautiful painterly effects. **4**

The porous clay surface is very receptive, and more forgiving than paper. If you don't like the results, simply give the offending area a bit of a scrub with a stiff, wet brush and wipe it off with a dampened sponge, until you've lightened the spot sufficiently to work over it again.

Even when working with thicker applications of underglazes in a direct painterly manner, you can blend colors in a wet-on-wet style. You might, for instance, want to use thicker applications of underglaze to cover a clay body color you don't like. Or you may just prefer the juicier, expressionistic look that a thicker underglaze application has to offer. **5**

Watercolor: A Brief Review

True to its name, watercolor painting uses water as the carrier for pigment. Because the water renders the pigment transparent, the color of the paper below shows through and affects the tint of the paint. Watercolor can produce crisp effects when painted on dry paper. On the other hand, hauntingly beautiful and ephemeral images can be created with a technique called *wet-on-wet*. After soaking large areas of the paper with water, the artist adds pigment directly onto the wet surface, blending colors and allowing strokes to bloom and spread as they will. Experience and chance play a large part in creating a watercolor-on-paper masterpiece. A misplaced stroke or an errant bloom of color cannot be washed out of the paper without tearing it up. A bisque clay surface can receive similar techniques, but it is way more forgiving, because the surface can be scrubbed to at least lighten, if not erase, errant marks.

When the blending of colors is complete and the surface is dry, crisper details can be added. **6**

Feeling the need to create a subtle framing effect, I brushed a single sweeping stroke along each edge of this tile.

OXIDES

Raw coloring oxides have a limited range of colors, but you can increase that range with washes and color gradients. When making an oxide wash, add just a small amount of commercial clear glaze to the water before mixing in the oxide. The binders in the glaze will help harden the oxide to the surface, in both the green and the fired state. Without the glaze, the diluted oxide would easily dust off and smear while handling. **7**

A very light coat of clear glaze was applied before firing. This hardened the oxide to the tile and imparted a slight shimmer to the surface, while allowing the character of the clay to show through.

PAINTING DETAILED IMAGES

With undiluted underglaze, you can create detailed naturalistic images with a great deal of depth and detail by developing your painting in layers, working again from light to dark, and from background to foreground. After sketching or transferring your image onto the piece, start to fill in the solid background shapes within your image. You'll want an even, opaque coating, which usually means applying three coats of the underglaze colors. This part of the image-developing process I liken to working with tempera paints. Choose only light to midrange colors for these areas, saving the darker tones for overlaying details.

As you paint, the underglaze will cover up your sketched guidelines, so you may have to redraw them after the underglaze is dry. If you used the transfer method, you can reposition your tracing paper image over your piece again and retransfer the details. **8**

If the painted shapes seem rather flat, you can add depth and bring the picture to life by shading and texturing with washes and a fan brush, as I did here. **9**

Details can be painted in with translucent underglazes. **10**

DESIGN CONSIDERATIONS

As I continued to add details, the image
came into sharper focus, but all that
visual activity in the center left the
border looking rather barren. I needed
to develop some textural interest there
to balance the frame with the image. I
used a fan brush to simulate the texture
of wood, then shaded the four dots
to make them look like dimensional
wooden plugs. The whole tile was then
clear glazed and fired.

**Note how the firing of the tile with a coat of clear glaze intensified
the underglaze colors from their raw state, while at the same time,
some of the transluscent overpainted details have become more
subdued. With practice and familiarity with materials, you can
learn to gauge which colors work best and how heavily to apply
them to get the desired results after the glaze firing.**

FINISHING SUGGESTIONS

Underglaze work, especially multicolored work, shows off best with a
clear or light-toned transparent glaze.
On the other hand, when showing
a bit of clay and working with color
that contrasts with it, translucent and
semiopaque glazes can also produce
interesting results. Vitreous-type
underglazes look great unglazed, as do
some oxides. Oxides as well as some
underglazes can be brushed in a thin
wash over a glaze and then fired.

Drawing with Underglaze Pencils and Crayons

FOR BISQUE WARE

If you've worked with soft pastels and pastel pencils on paper, underglaze crayons and pencils will feel somewhat familiar, although the ceramic versions are much denser and harder. If your only contact with pastels has been to admire them, you'll be happy to know that the unmistakable line quality of chalk and pencil shines through.

▼ **Materials**

Underglaze pencils, underglaze crayons

Get acquainted with underglaze pencils and crayons (also called *chalks*) on a light-colored scrap of bisque. Draw, scribble, smudge, and blend. You can use them over any color you wish, but a light surface will give you a better sense of their true colors. **1**

The two practice tiles were first bisqued to affix the loose chalk lines, then clear glazed and refired.

RELATED TECHNIQUES

Brushwork

For a richer effect, you can draw over a base coat of bisqued-on underglaze. Bold linear elements yield dramatic contrast. For a subtler effect, smudge the lines into a soft, even tone.

When creating dimensional images, it's best to develop your shading by working from light colors to dark. For these images, the undercoat of liquid underglaze should be a light to medium color, to allow the darker, drawn elements to show over them.

FINISHING SUGGESTIONS

Underglaze crayons and pencils remain rather chalky and dusty on the surface of your piece. So before proceeding further it's best to fire your piece yet another time, to a bisque temperature, to affix the chalk. You can just stick it into your next bisque firing. After that, you can follow the finishing suggestions on page 79. For the tile, I used a clear glaze over the chalk decoration.

Trailing with Underglaze

FOR BISQUE WARE

Filled with underglaze, trailing tools with fine-tipped pen nibs can be used almost like fine line markers to draw fine, sharp lines of varying width. They're great for illustrative drawing, for writing, and for adding details to underglaze brushwork. You can work with brilliant color or experiment with black-trailed lines and a gray wash, a method that mimics the traditional "works-on-paper" technique of a pen and ink wash.

▼ **Tools**

Trailing tools with pen nibs, brush, watercolor palette

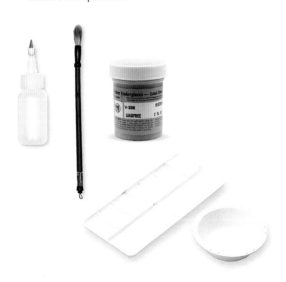

Once clear glazed and fired, the colors darkened and intensified.

For basic instructions on using trailing bottles, review "Trailing with Slip," page 61, but note two differences. First, when drawing with underglaze, your trailing tools will need pen nibs; a simple squeeze bottle won't do. Second, those nibs are especially prone to clogging. Most come with a small cleaning wire; shooting clean water out of the tip, using a spare bottle, also works. **1**

As you draw your lines, don't scrape the tip hard against the surface; just barely touch it. Because this is a precise technique, it's a particularly good idea to have guidelines to follow. (See "Transferring to Bisque," page 30.)

You can draw an image entirely by trailing, or combine it with areas of painted underglaze.  We used a similar combination when drawing with chalk, but the results were quite different. Turn to photo 3 on page 81, and compare.

A second comparison: Chalk lines can be softened by blending, but, drawn in pen, the turquoise lines will remain crisp and definitive.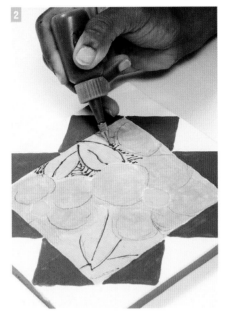

DESIGN CONSIDERATIONS

A transparent turquoise glaze was painted over the areas with radiating turquoise lines, subduing their visual energy just enough to allow the clear glazed center to pop with dominating exuberance.

FINISHING SUGGESTIONS

Follow the finishing suggestions on page 79.

WORKING IN BLACK AND WHITE

A composition in black and white can be stunning. Browse through some images of pen and ink drawings and black and white engravings from master artists. Note the distribution of dark and light tones, and how the artist uses them to define form. Remember, dark tones recede into the shadows, while light tones advance toward the viewer.

With this in mind, analyze your prepared image, and consider where the lights, darks, and midrange tones should be. With a fine line marker, define the lines that will be drawn with the trailing tool. Then use a pencil to shade the areas where your wash will be.

Make a range of washes with black

underglaze and water, and brush them onto scrap bisque to gauge their effects. **4**

Transfer your image to the piece, and then use a trailing tool to draw the linear elements in your design. If you like the crisp linear image just as it is, feel free to stop here. **5**

Guided by the shading in your plan

drawing, begin laying in the various tones, working from light to dark, gradually increasing the concentration of black in your wash, and coaxing the appropriate parts of your image to emerge from or recede into the surface. If you darken an area too much, give it a bit of a scrub with a stiff wet brush to loosen it, then either spread the wash around or wipe it up. 6

DESIGN CONSIDERATIONS

Although I had shaded the entire space around the flowers, I felt the panel needed to be defined more sharply with a ruled edge. With ruled lines in place, I was better able to determine what else was needed to complete the border. 7

I drew energetic little flecks on the border to create an overall texture, and blended yellow, orange, and red glazes for the petals, plus various shades of green for the leaves and stem. The border got a coat of translucent glaze in deep turquoise; the center, a clear one. The black and white background contrasts beautifully with the colorful areas, thus emphasizing the central floral bouquet.

▦ FINISHING SUGGESTIONS

This "pen and ink" method can

> ▶ **Tip:** When using a ruler as a paint guide, choose one with an elevated edge, rather than one that lies flush with the surface. This will prevent your color from oozing and spreading under the ruler.

be finished with a solid coating of a transparent glaze or transformed into a multicolor composition with the application of transparent glazes in various tints.

Masking and Stenciling with Sponging, Spattering, and Spraying

FOR BISQUE WARE

Masking and stenciling cover and protect selected areas to maintain the color that lies underneath. Sponging, spattering, and spraying, which tend to scatter color in all directions, often benefit from being masked. They also add great visual texture to your work.

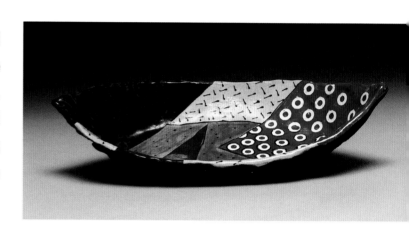

◀ **Tools and Materials**

Scissors, craft knife, newsprint, stickers, clear self-adhesive paper, masking tape, card stock, paper, stencils, hake brush

▮ MASKING

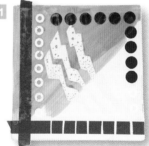

Like wax resist, masking is a resist technique. Now that we're working with underglazes on bisque, we have a bigger arsenal of materials and methods at our disposal. Many masking materials have sticky backs, which are easy to use on vertical pieces. Clear, self-adhesive shelf paper is handy. Simply cut out your shape, adhere it to your ceramic piece, and brush on your underglaze. (Or use any of the techniques below.) **1**

Before pulling off the masks, allow the color to dry slightly; it should be firm but still slightly damp. Otherwise, flakes of underglaze will come off along with the masks. **2**

Unlike wax resist, masking materials can be removed and replaced with other masks, allowing you to develop a complex composition without too much trouble.

The masking materials allowed the off-white clay color to show through in the design. To unify the tile and disguise an anemic clay color, I coated the tile with a transparent pink glaze and fired it.

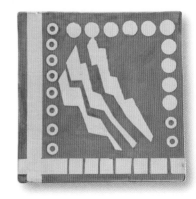

RELATED TECHNIQUES

Resists for Slip Decoration

Here I begin our project with just two strips of masking tape, creating two white bands along the sides.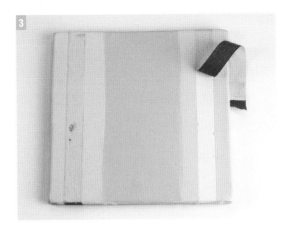

Perforated papers (think doilies and lace paper) make excellent masks, leaving behind beautiful and complex textures. A large doily covers most of the tile at left. At right, you can see the white line from the masking tape on the right-hand border beginning to establish multiple layers of depth as I paint over a piece of lace paper.

A paper doily shielded the white areas from the blue underglaze that I brushed on. When the color was dry, I applied a clear glaze to the tile before firing it.

STENCILS

Stencils are another means of masking your work; they are especially handy in that they are reusable. There are a multitude of images and shapes available commercially, plus you can make your own from heavy card stock, a sheet of transparent matte acetate film, or Mylar. Just transfer your image to the stencil material—a manila folder works well for the flower shown—and cut out the openings with a craft knife.

▶ **Tools**

Stencil brushes

Hold your stencil in place and apply your underglaze. The best way is to dab it on with a sponge or stencil brush. If you brush it on with a regular brush, take care that a stray hair doesn't slip under the stencil, leaving an errant mark.

SPONGING

Sponging—oh so simple, but what a variety of textural effects it can achieve!

Inexpensive sponges are available in a wide choice of natural and synthetic materials, each producing its own characteristic effect. The natural sea varieties tend to have open and irregular textures, offering a variety of results from the same sponge. Ceramic suppliers carry a few synthetic sponges with their own unique texture. Household cellulose and synthetic sponges offer yet more choices.

Live it up! Try them all, Dab, stamp, and sweep back and forth in short, brushlike strokes to see what textures they can make. Increase their versatility by cutting them down to different sizes or specific shapes.

To charge your sponge with color, you can spread a thin layer of underglaze on an impervious surface and dip your sponge into it. Or you can brush color (or several colors) directly onto the sponge. **7**

Feel free to combine—and adapt— commercial and hand-cut stencils. In the center of my large handmade-stenciled flower, I've added some stamens by sponging over a commercial stencil of an intricate flower. **8**

▶ **Tools**

Sponges

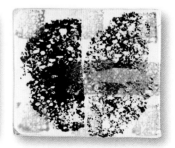

By adding layers of color, sponging can either tone down or brighten a composition. These tiles here were clear glazed and fired.

RELATED TECHNIQUES

Pop-up Sponges

Pop-up sponges start out thin and get thick fast when wet, hence the name. In their thin state, they can be easily cut to shape with ordinary scissors, then "popped up" and used as decorative stamps.

Even better, they're available in large, inexpensive sheets at art and craft stores. Just draw your design with a permanent marker, and cut it out with scissors. If you insist on tight details, they can be shaped with a craft knife. Tiny sewing scissors can snip details into the popped-up surface. **9**

Design Considerations

The blank area above and below the central flower appeared a bit inactive. It needed something to contribute to the visual flow. I decided to add a small dot to echo all the circular forms in the design, providing unity. Additionally, the two dots help frame the composition. **10**

■ SPATTERING

▶ **Tools**
Toothbrush, spatter brush

charge your brush, dip it directly into the color, or dab color on more judiciously with another brush. If you're developing a multicolor texture, be sure to clean your brush well between colors. **11**

Spattering offers its own textural opportunities. Color is flicked, or spattered, onto the surface in small droplets until the desired density is attained.

A stiff-bristled brush (try a toothbrush) works best. Simply strike your thumb across the color-loaded brush while holding it close to the work. Spatter layers of different colors for richer, more variegated effects. To

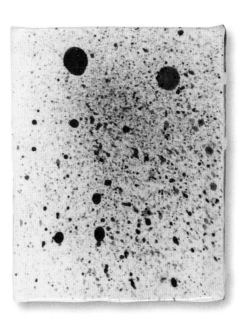

A spattered pattern can be quite haphazard, with irregularly sized spots and uneven color density, creating an energetic textural effect. The tile was clear glazed and fired.

Design Considerations

To add even more interest to the areas above and below the central flower, I decided to spatter a few colors that harmonize with the bluish green below. I didn't want my stamens or lace paper bands to be affected, so I masked them with pieces of paper. **12**

■ SPRAYING

Spraying underglaze onto a ceramic surface can produce a variety of results depending on the tool used. An *airbrush* delivers fine, perfectly even layers of color, subtle blushes, and amazingly smooth gradations, leaving no stroke marks. However, the tool is finicky, complicated, and pricey. Luckily, there are simpler and cheaper tools that can give you results almost as good.

A low-tech option is the mechanical mouth atomizer. The ones with their own reservoir and plastic tubing for a mouthpiece are the most convenient for maneuvering around three-dimensional work. Just fill the reservoir with a thinned-down solution of underglaze, aim, and blow. The solution should be free of lumps and the consistency of whole milk or thinner, depending on the saturation of the color you want.

Spraying can create a range of surfaces, from perfectly even to soft and ephemeral. The tile was clear glazed and fired.

▼ Tools
Atomizers

If the atomizer you have is of the simple-hinged, dual-tube variety, then merely open the atomizer until it stops at a right angle, put the long skinny tube into the fluid, and blow into the end of the shorter tube. The liquid is reduced to a fine spray and comes out at the juncture point. **13**

RELATED TECHNIQUES

Resists for Slip Decoration

Design Considerations

Using my original flower template and a few other pieces of paper to mask and protect previous work, I sprayed the tips of the petals to darken and accentuate them.

When the masks were removed, I discovered that the spattering had obscured my blue-green dots. Once they were restamped, the design finally felt complete.

FINISHING SUGGESTIONS

Follow the finishing suggestions on page 79. To finish the tile, I simply clear glazed and fired it.

Staining

FOR BISQUE WARE

To stain, or *patina*, a surface is to subtly alter the natural color of the clay and intensify the texture you have created. A watered-down solution of a ceramic stain, oxide, underglaze, or even glaze is layered onto the porous bisque until the desired intensity of color is achieved. Results can range from soft and subtle on smooth surfaces to bold and dynamic on textured ones.

▶ **Tools**

Brushes, sponge

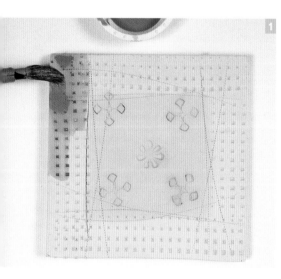

IF YOU'VE EVER STAINED WOOD, you know that the color and tone of the finished project depend on the color and intensity of the stain, as well as the original color of the wood itself. The same is true of ceramic surfaces. In photo 1, for example, the anemic pink tone of the clay interacts with washes of yellow and green underglaze to produce a distinctive color. **1**

To make a stain, place a small amount of coloring material in a plastic container or watercolor cup, and slowly add water until you have a solution that is watery, yet still has the intensity of color you desire. Test by dabbing a bit on a scrap of bisque, and add more water or material as needed.

Staining smooth surfaces can be attractive, but it's when staining is applied to textured surfaces that a perfect union is found. Staining adds emphasis to even the subtlest of textural surfaces, showing off all the incising or impressing you did at the wet ware or leather-hard stage. Darker colors that contrast with the clay show up best, and you'll want to mix your stain to the deepest intensity possible while keeping it fluid. Brush the stain onto the surface, making sure that it gets into every crevice. A natural-bristled utility brush works well. **2**

Let the stain dry completely. Then don a pair of rubber gloves and carefully wipe it off the raised areas with a dampened sponge. You'll begin to see the richness of your surface texture come through. Keep a container of water nearby, and rinse out the sponge frequently as you work. On very shallow textures, where a damp sponge may eliminate too much color, try using a dry paper towel. **3**

DESIGN CONSIDERATIONS

After bisquing the tinted tile shown in photo 1, I used a deep blue stain to accentuate the texture. The blue also created harmony, because it further tinted the yellow and green areas, leaving them unified yet still distinct from each other. **4**

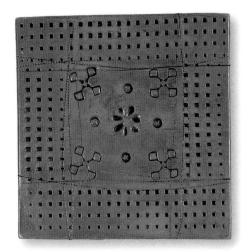

FINISHING SUGGESTIONS

Staining could well be the last of your decorative steps. Left unglazed and simply fired, stained work can be stunning on textured surfaces and gorgeously subdued on smooth ones. Applying a clear, transparent or translucent glaze also works. For example, the tile at right has a glossy, light yellow glaze; the one below has a translucent matte glaze.

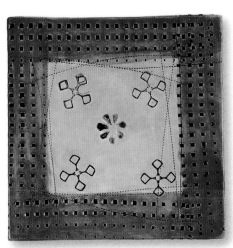

Textures like the ones in these stamp and roulette decorated tiles can be emphasized by staining with a contrasting colored material.

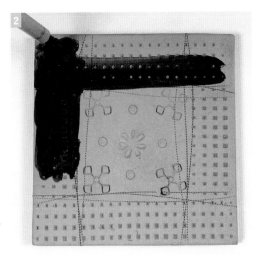

Gallery

Jenny Mendes
Vases, 2009

Average height, 5½ inches (14 cm) tall
Hand-built Stan's clay from Highwater Clays;
hand-painted layers of custom terra sigillatas;
electric fired, cone 03
Photo by Bob Barrett

George Bowes
Folded Vase: Dappled Basket Weave, 2009

10 x 5½ inches (25.4 x 14 cm)
Thrown and altered porcelain; underglazes,
glazes; cone 5
Photos by artist

Sandra Zeiset Richardson
The Secret, 1997

24½ x 17 x 6¾ inches (62.2 x 43.2 x 1.7.1 cm)
Hand-built low-fire white clay; carved relief;
low-fire underglazes applied to greenware
before bisque firing, black underglaze applied
to surface and sponge manipulated, clear matte
glaze then applied and fired; electric fired, bisque
and underglazes cone 05, glazes, cone 04
Photos by Stan Richardson

Laurie Shaman
Winged Vase, 2007

14 x 14 x 3 inches (35.6 x 35.6 x 7.6 cm)
Hand-built porcelain; incised; electric fired,
cone 06; sgraffito, slip trail, brushwork of
underglazes; clear glaze; cone 6
Photos by Peter Kiar

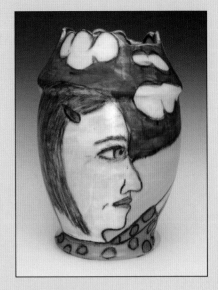

Wendy Olson
Cat Charmer, 2009

14 x 7 x 7 inches (35.6 x 17.8 x 17.8 cm)
Hand-built and wheel-thrown white stoneware;
underglaze pencil; underglaze with matte clear
glaze fired to cone 6 electric
Photo by artist

Frank Gaydos
Platter Hex, 2008

Diameter, 26 inches (66 cm)
Hump mold-formed and thrown
terra-cotta; tape resist; glazed
cone 04
Photos by Arthur Danek

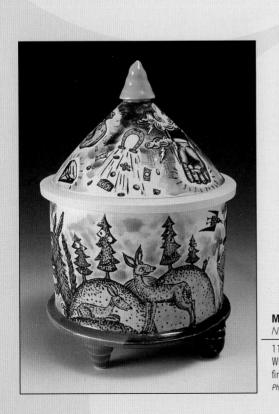

Michael Corney
Nature, 2006

11 x 8 x 8 inches (27.9 x 20.3 x 20.3 cm)
Wheel-thrown porcelain; brush painted; electric
fired, cone 10; glaze, stains, underglaze
Photo by artist

Working with Glazes

Glazes—the luscious icing on a ceramic layer cake. A surface so diverse, visual, and tactile, so rich with depth and articulation, exceeding any paint in its brilliance and durability. Glaze can really bring all the layers together.

■ SELECTING GLAZES

Glazes are defined by two characteristics: their degree of transmittance, which pertains to how well you can see through the glaze to what's beneath, and their surface texture.

Transmittance

From the most to the least transmittant, glazes can be clear, transparent, translucent, semiopaque, or opaque.

A **clear glaze** should be just that— clear, with no tinting or fogging, offering a pure, clean view to what is below. It's the best choice for a multicolor decoration if you want the original colors to remain true but become more intense. Some low-fire clear glazes can get a bit milky when applied too thickly, so be sure to apply the glaze evenly.

A **transparent glaze** is a clear base glaze with added colorants. What lies below can be easily seen, but it is tinted, similar to the effect of looking through tinted sunglasses or through a piece of colored cellophane. This tinting can, if wisely color matched, greatly enhance images and clay surfaces, uniting them to each other as well as to the form.

A **translucent glaze** makes everything a bit hazier. Usually only contrasting tones will show up well, although such subtlety can make for quite an attractive effect.

A **semiopaque glaze** has a lot of covering power, but not 100 percent. You won't see the color of most clays, but some contrasting marks may bleed through.

▶ **Tip:** Some clear glazes can adversely affect the color of the decoration underneath, especially if the color is green, which may be transformed into brown. Be sure to test all clear glazes over all colors, but be especially vigilant with green.

A very dark clay may bleed through enough to affect the color of the glaze. If you want to block that, you can lay down a coat of white underglaze prior to glazing. Alternatively, you may want to use a totally opaque glaze instead.

An **opaque glaze** blocks any colors at all from bleeding through.

■ SURFACE TEXTURE

Glazes are also classified according to their surfaces. A *gloss* glaze is shiny, a *satin* one a bit less so, with just a slight sheen. *Matte* glazes have no sheen at all but do have a smooth surface, though some matte surfaces are a bit pithier than others. A *dry* glaze resembles bisque—dry and slightly rough.

Textured glazes include a broad range of surfaces, from crawled to cratered to crackled—all attributes that might be considered defects for functional ware, but which make for fascinating surfaces when used on sculpture or decorative forms. In general, textured, matte, and dry surfaces are best for sculptural work, because shiny surfaces tend to reflect light, making it hard to see the sculpture's form.

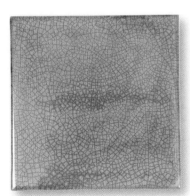

Pooling

Some glazes change color from thick to thin applications, which affects the way they interact with the form. They pool or accumulate more thickly in the deeper recesses of a texture, usually becoming darker in the low spots and lighter in the high ones, though the reverse may be true with some particular glazes. They're excellent choices for highly textured pieces.

Glaze Charts

Commercial glaze manufacturers offer glaze color charts to aid in your selection. They are available through your ceramic supply shop, sometimes for a small charge, or you can view the colors online. Most shops have charts with actual glazed ceramic chips as samples, so you can get a better feel for what the glaze looks like. But be sure to test on your own clay body, because the results may very well differ a bit. For example, a glaze will look different over a dark clay than over a light one.

■ GLAZE DEFECTS

When it comes to glazing and firing, even the best-laid plans can produce mystifying results. Commercial glazes give fairly consistent results—and of course you tried them out on your test tiles!—but other factors can make a glaze fail. Here are a few common flaws, along with some tips for sleuthing out a solution.

Crazing is a network of fine cracks **1**. It is caused by an improper fit, a glaze that is in tension with the clay. Glazes on an underfired clay body can often develop a crackle or crazing pattern as the porous ware absorbs ambient moisture and expands beyond the ability of the glaze. This disparate expansion and contraction causes the cracks.

The effect is often deliberately sought as a decorative effect, and even accentuated by rubbing a dark material such as ink into the crackle glazes to simulate an antiqued appearance. This can work beautifully for exterior or sculptural work, but crazing is not suitable for contact with food, because the tiny cracks make the surface unsanitary.

If you don't want this effect, make sure your clay and your glaze mature at compatible temperatures. If they don't, either choose another clay body or find another glaze. An alternative is to bisque fire high, to the maturing temperature of the clay, then glaze fire to the lower temperature of the glaze. Crazing can also be minimized or prevented by slowing down the kiln cooling process, and not opening the lid until the kiln has cooled to about 200°F (93°C).

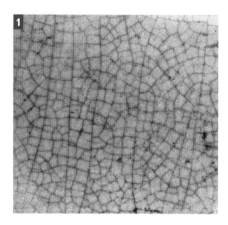

Crawling happens during the melting process, when the glaze cracks, pulls apart, and rolls back on itself, leaving bare spots of exposed clay **2**. The effect can be slight or so severe that the glaze beads up into a fairly uniform texture. Raw glazes naturally tend to shrink a bit as they dry on the surface. Fluid glazes will heal themselves in the firing, but certain stiffer glazes, especially when applied too thickly, will develop cracks that do not heal and thus will crawl. A glaze may also crawl if the ware is not washed before glazing, and dust or grease remains on the surface, thereby interfering with the glaze-to-clay bond.

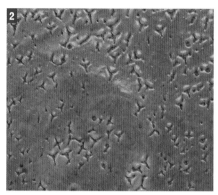

Pinholing develops when air bubbles in the molten glaze burst and don't have time to heal, leaving behind a network of tiny holes or pits in the glaze surface **3**. Applying a thinner layer of glaze and extending the length of firing, by holding the temperature at its highest point for a *soaking period*, give the glaze more time to melt and heal.

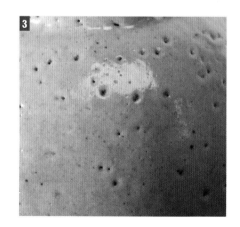

HELPFUL TO REVIEW

Washes	Making a Gradient	Brushing	Brushes	Making Test Tiles	Dipping	Pouring
76	**76**	**31**	**23**	**28**	**31**	**32**

Blistering occurs when bubbles, or the craters of burst bubbles, are left behind on the surface [4]. The glaze has not had time to smooth out before it cools and sets. A glaze can blister when it's applied too thickly, as in the bottom of bowls, where it has been allowed to pool. A thinner application and a soaking of the kiln at the top firing temperature can help fix the problem.

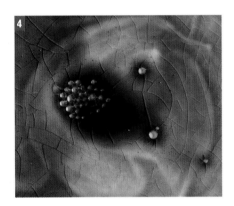

Other defects may result from incorrect firing. If the glaze surface comes out unexpectedly rough and scratchy, then the ware was probably underfired. Overfired ware will be excessively shiny, and the glaze may have run down to the lower parts of the work, or even onto the kiln shelf itself. Check firing settings and make sure they are correct. Also, some kilns can fire unevenly due to poor design or to uneven packing of ware. Place cone packs at different spots in the kiln to determine whether your kiln is firing evenly.

■ EXPERIMENTING

Now that you've surveyed your choices, don't just go straight to the gloss glazes and nowhere else. Try mixing it up a bit. Setting one kind of surface up against a contrasting one brings a lot of textural interest and variety to your work.

Experiment with different surface types as well as techniques. Many of the slip and underglaze techniques presented earlier can be utilized with glazes, too. One glaze can be stamped or sponged on top of another. A glaze can be combed or trailed. All of the resist and masking processes can also be utilized. The possibilities are endless.

We'll begin to incorporate some of those methods as we introduce a technique called *majolica*, in which ceramic stains are painted directly onto the raw surface of a white opaque glaze. The segment on layering will get you started using different glazes together, over or under each other, utilizing some earlier techniques in the process.

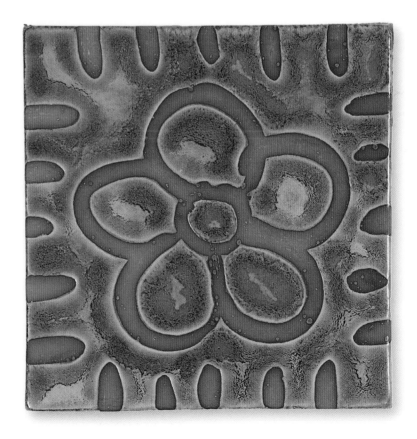

Majolica

FOR BISQUE WARE

Majolica is a wonderfully versatile glaze technique that is capable of both fluid, painterly expression and clean, crisp effects. A raw (unfired) layer of opaque white glaze is your canvas. Your paints are translucent: glaze stains, coloring oxides, watered-down underglazes, or specially formulated majolica colors.

▼ **Tools**

Brushes, sgraffito tools

■ THE BASE

The first step is to apply the base majolica glaze to your ware. If you're working with a commercial glaze (sensible for beginners), just brush it on, following the instructions on the label.

On the other hand, a homemade majolica glaze (see the recipe on page 123) should be either dipped or poured. Homemade glazes are not very fluid, so brush strokes usually show up in the fired piece.

Because applying the base is a bit of a production, and because it needs to dry before you continue, best practice is to glaze all your pieces at one time and let them sit for a day before proceeding. Be sure to glaze a few scraps of bisque while you're at it. **1**

RELATED TECHNIQUES

Brushwork with Underglaze and Oxides	Sgraffito with Slip	Sponging	Spattering	Masking and Stenciling	Wax Resist
75	61	88	89	86-87	33

■ THE COLORS

Special majolica colors are available commercially. They come ready-mixed in a broad range of colors and are easy to use. I definitely recommend them for beginners. Even professional artists have incorporated them into their palettes, lured by consistent results and timesaving efficiency.

Should you want to try making your own, instructions for using coloring oxides and stains are included on page 123. Handmade majolica stains can be used in the same piece with commercial colors. You just need to test, as always, to make sure the stain has the proper amount of flux for your temperature range.

Alternatively, many commercial underglazes, and even some glazes, can be thinned down and used as majolica colors. Be sure to test them before trying them out on a special piece. Underglazes in particular might be too refractory and thus might fire with a dry finish. To remedy that, add some majolica glaze to the underglaze in a 1:3 or 1:4 ratio; it will act as a fluxing agent.

Firing the tiles brought out some subtleties in the brushwork and some minor shifts in color, but they remained pretty close to their raw appearance.

■ APPLYING THE COLOR

Majolica is an extremely versatile process, happy to accept masking, sponging, spattering, spraying, and sgraffito. Because the applied colors will fuse into the base glaze, results tend to be a bit softer and more subdued than their underglaze equivalents. **2**

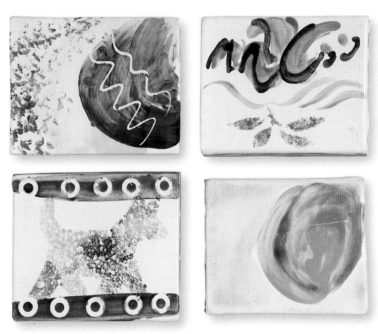

But it is with brushwork that majolica truly shines. Choose soft-haired brushes. Ideal for painterly approaches are Oriental bamboo brushes, whose soft, springy bristles hold a lot of material but keep a fine point. When testing your colors, play around with different strokes to see what you and your brushes can do. Pointers on washes and gradients are found on page 76, should you want a refresher. **3**

Brushing color directly onto that raw white glaze can be a rather unforgiving venture. Misplaced brush strokes are not easily removed. Your only options are to incorporate the error into the design or wash the white glaze off the entire piece and start over. To help avoid this, sketch your design in pencil or transfer it to your ware (see page 30) before applying color.

If a direct, painterly approach is what you're after, practice your brushwork first with watercolor on paper, to figure out how you want to layer your colors. Then brush your image onto your ware with watered-down food coloring. It will burn out in the firing. I like to start with yellow, then add drops of red as I get surer of my placement and ready to define my lines. Use the colors that work best for you. **4**

With guidelines in place, painting can begin. Working from light to dark, lay in the larger background areas first. Because you're working with translucent paints, overlapping colors will show through and interact, so you can shade, highlight, or accentuate parts of your form by over-brushing a stroke or two in a different color. **5**

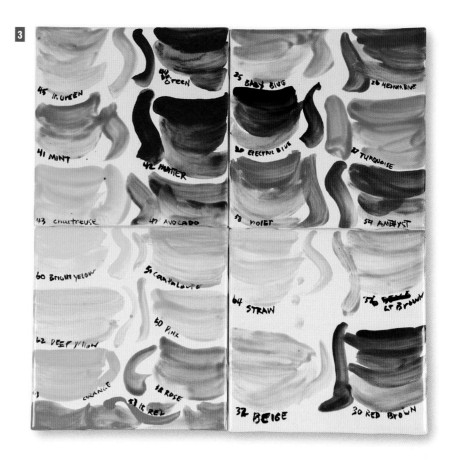

■ DESIGN CONSIDERATIONS

Before going any further with the central flower, I wanted to define the border. With a small dagger brush, I began to develop a scrolling frame, echoing the fluid, painterly style of the lily. **6**

Wax resist can be painted over decorative elements to shield them from additional layers of color. I waxed over my scrolled lines in preparation for painting the border and background. **7**

With the lines protected, I used a broad brush to apply a smooth, even coat of color around the border, without having to worry about overstepping my edges. **8**

Once the brushwork is complete, accents can be added with sgraffito. Remember that the base glaze is white, which is what your etched lines will be. On the project tile, a few white lines added a bit of emphasis around the flower and on the petals. **9**

■ FIRING

With brushwork and sgraffito complete, the piece is ready to fire to the maturing temperature of the base majolica glaze. Because it's not a very fluid glaze, majolica firings benefit from a soaking period toward the end of the firing. Fifteen to 30 minutes is usually sufficient—less time for commercial glazes, more for homemade.

Layering

FOR BISQUE WARE

When glazes are applied as independent layers in their raw state, they meld together in the firing, producing interesting and sometimes surprising color combinations and textural effects.

▼ Tools

Masking and stencil materials, brushes, sponges

■ TESTING AND EXPERIMENTING

The only way—and I mean the *only* way—to know how glazes will interact with each other is to test them: to make your own test tiles. Here's an efficient way to do that.

Select a few base (background) glazes to test; for instance, a light glaze and a dark one in both gloss and matte, a couple of fluid transparent glazes, and perhaps some textured ones. Apply each glaze to half a tile. Here I'm testing four base glazes: a gloss white, a matte black, a fluid textured turquoise, and a transparent amber.

After the tiles are dry, brush on a flowing stroke of a different glaze across the background glaze and down into the unglazed area below. Use as many glazes as will fit across the tile. Go for variety, including glazes with contrasting characteristics to the base glaze—for example, a gloss over a matte and vice versa.

When the glaze strokes are dry, brush another coat of the background glaze over the lower half of the tile, to see how that glaze reacts when applied over the others as well as under them. **1**

Don't forget to keep track of each glaze you test. Use an underglaze pencil to label the back of each tile so you will be able to repeat your results—or not.

When fired, tests may produce everything from gorgeous gems to dismal duds. It's better to find out now. **2**

If you're looking for excitement, there are special texturing glazes available that, when applied over or under other glazes, combine with them to turn into a textured glaze. Most come in white, which can be tinted to your desired shade with underglaze colors. **3**

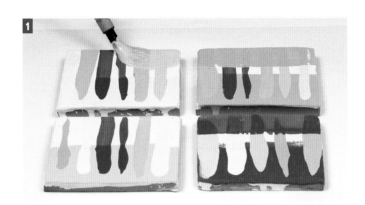

■ APPLICATION

Many of the techniques described earlier are great ways to layer glazes. Brushing, sponging, masking, stenciling, pouring, trailing, wax resist—all are excellent candidates. To illustrate the possibilities, follow along as I create a sample tile, using a variation of the design that appeared in "Masking and Stenciling with Sponging, Spattering, and Spraying" on page 86, with several different techniques.

Note: Because I wanted a white base to work on, I applied a layer of white slip to my red clay tile at the leather-hard stage, before bisque firing it.

Tips for Layering Glazes

1 When fluid transparent glazes are layered, results will mostly be a soft-edged blending of colors. You'll probably get what you'd expect from paint. For example, a yellow glaze over a medium blue one is likely to look greenish. But chemical reactions can slip you a surprise. So test, test, test.

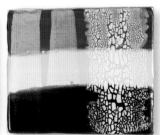

2 To get the most interesting reactions, overlap glazes with differing characteristics. For instance, an opaque, light-colored glaze might visually percolate up through a dark, translucent glaze in an interesting way.

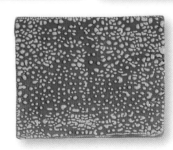

3 Reactions often vary depending on whether one glaze is over or under the other, so include both versions in your testing.

Using masking tape to block out the center of the tile, I laid in a band of orchid matte glaze along each side of the tile. Once that was dry, I placed a strip of masking tape down the middle of each band of orchid to shield it from the next layer of glaze. **4**

Next I layered a dark purple matte glaze over the orchid. Because these are both from the same glaze series, made from same base glaze, I didn't expect any significant interaction. **5**

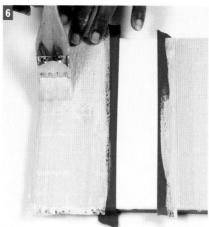

To create some textural interest along the bordering bands, I applied one coat of a texturing glaze over strips of lace paper. When the glaze was dry, the lace paper was removed. **6**

Now it was time to lay in the background glazes for the central band. To protect the purple bands, I first applied masking tape over their edges. **7**

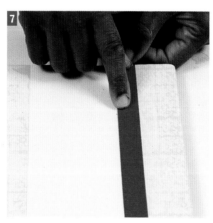

I sought to create a central focal area with a distinct and lighter glaze than that on the ends of the central band. To do that, I made a circle stencil to shield the space, and applied a darker glaze on both ends of the central band. **8**

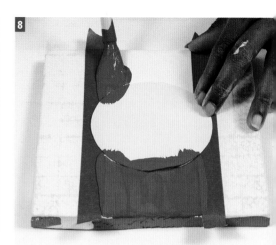

After the glaze was dry, I removed the circle stencil and replaced it with the negative area of a slightly larger circle stencil. This way, the glaze in my central circle would overlap and interact with the surrounding area, creating a bit of a halo. **9**

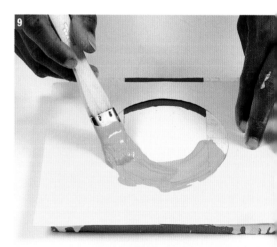

With that complete, it was time to develop my central flower. Reusing the flower stencil from the "Masking and Stenciling with Sponging, Spattering, and Spraying" section (page 86), I used a foam stencil brush to first work in a matte green glaze, and then a gloss green glaze on top. 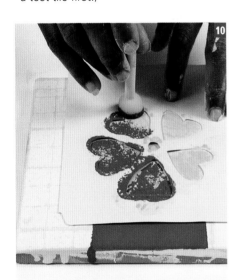 (I know it looks rust-colored now, but it fires to a glossy green. Many of the raw colorants used in glazes change dramatically in the firing, so don't be alarmed if the color in the jar is totally different from the sample on the glaze chart. But as always, when in doubt, do a test tile first.)

My final step was to add a bit of texture to the dark background. I also wanted a dot in the area, so I used a sticky label as a mask. Shielding the flower and the sides with pieces of paper, I used a natural sponge to apply a texturing glaze to create a gradient.

Make sure you keep thorough notes of all the different layers and placement of glaze. Once out of the kiln, results may be difficult to decipher, and you'll want to be able to repeat the successes and learn what not to do from your less than satisfactory examples.

Gallery

Ronan Kyle Peterson
Slug Weevil Teapot, 2009

8 x 10 x 6 inches (20.3 x 25.4 x 15.2 cm)
Wheel-thrown, altered, and assembled red earthenware;
white slip, slip-trailed dots, red terra sigillata with wax
resist; alkaline, textured glasses; electric kiln, cone 03
Photo by Fancy Rondo

George Bowes
Flower Brick, 2006

6 x 5 inches (15.2 x 12.7 cm)
Thrown and altered porcelain; underglazes,
glazes, cone 5
Photo by artist

Linda Arbuckle
Bowl: Fall Dreams of Spring, 2008

10 x 4 inches (25.4 x 10.2 cm)
Thrown terra-cotta; majolica; oxidation fired,
cone 003
Photo by artist

Susan DeMay
Commuting with Nature, 2004

17¼ x 17¼ x 1½ inches (43.8 x 43.8 x 3.8 cm)
Slab-built and press-molded stoneware; wax and
tape resist; cone 6 glazes; electric fired, cone 6
Photo by John Lucas

Jeff Reich
Greythorn, 2009

11 x 14 x 7 inches (27.9 x 35.6 x 17.8 cm)
Hand-built black stoneware; reduction fired, cone 10;
glaze sgraffito, crawling, shino glaze
Photo by artist

Lynn Smiser Bowers
Pitcher with Butterfly, 2008

10 x 9 x 7 inches (25.4 x 22.9 x 17.8 cm)
Wheel-thrown and hand-built porcelain; wax
resist, stencils, oxide brushwork; gas, reduction kiln, cone 10
Photos by artist

Posey Bacopoulos
Oil and Vinegar Set, 2007

6 x 12 x 5 inches (15.2 x 30.5 x 12.7 cm)
Wheel-thrown and altered terra-cotta; majolica with
painted stains, sgraffito; electric fired, cone 04
Photo by Kevin Nobel

Jeff Reich
Interwoven Fields, 2009

21 x 17 x 17 inches (53.3 x 43.2 x 43.2 cm)
Hand-built black stoneware; reduction fired, cone 10;
glaze sgraffito, crawling, shino glaze with 10% Mason
stains and Mayco hot tamale red fired to cone 10
Photo by artist

Post-Firing Techniques

FOR GLAZE-FIRED CLAY

Once your ware is glazed and fired, do you think it's all over but the shouting? Not necessarily. Perhaps the piece isn't quite what you wanted. Well, there's good news! There are decorating techniques that can take you beyond that first glaze firing.

Alyssa Welch
Flower Brick, 2008

4 x 5 x 6 inches (10.2 x 12.7 x 15.2 cm)
Slip-cast porcelain; cut vinyl resist; electric fired;
cone 6; sandblasted and luster fired
Photo by artist

▶ **Tools**
Brushes, decal squeegee

■ REGLAZING WITH CONVENTIONAL GLAZES

Suppose you find the glaze was not evenly applied, or you just don't like the way it looks. You can reglaze and refire the piece with the same glaze or with another, compatible glaze. A sound piece can be reglazed and refired an infinite number of times as long as all successive firings are at the same temperature or lower. If a later firing is higher in temperature, previous glaze results will be compromised, and the piece itself may lose its structural integrity.

Of course, the second time around is a bit trickier. Conventional glazes can grab onto a bisque surface because it's porous, which a glazed surface is not. To trick the second glaze into sticking, heat the piece in a kiln set on low, or in a warm house oven—250 to 300°F (121 to 149°C) should do—for 20 to 30 minutes, until it's just hot enough to require oven mitts or kiln gloves to handle. Remove it promptly and apply the new glaze while the piece is still warm. Heating is necessary only for this second coat. Subsequent coats will stick to those below, provided you don't disturb the base coat during application. Brush gently!

■ OVERGLAZING WITH DECORATIVE MATERIALS

Decals, china paints, and lusters are all on-glaze decorative materials that fire at very low temperatures—from cone 022 to cone 015. They aren't compatible with all glazes. Check the glaze label. In the absence of a reassuring "takes overglaze" or "luster compatible," assume the worst until you can get more information from the merchant or the manufacturer's website, or by testing the glaze yourself. When using homemade glazes, always test.

▶ **Tip:** Glazes that contain copper are usually unsuitable for on-glaze techniques, because copper reverts to a metallic black when it's refired at a lower temperature.

With all three materials, work in an area that's as clean and dust free as possible. Wash dust and oily residue off your ware with water, and clean it with rubbing alcohol just prior to decorating.

Decals

If you want detailed imagery or fine lettering but don't feel confident about executing them yourself, ceramic decals are just the thing. Check with a ceramic supply store or with online companies that specialize in ceramic decals. You'll find a huge selection. **1**

A ceramic decal is a silk-screened image made with china paints, printed onto the slick side of a specially made decal paper, and covered with a clear protective coat. When the painted image is removed from its paper backing, the cover coat holds it together. Sometimes this coat is tinted so you can see it more easily, both on and off the paper. The tint doesn't affect the finished look, because the cover coat burns off during firing.

A decal is easy to apply. Just cut it out and soak it in water. In a couple of minutes, when you can slide the image around on its paper backing, it's ready to apply. **2**

Wet your ceramic surface, so the decal will move around on it easily. Remove the decal from the water, and gently slide it off the backing and onto the ceramic piece. When you have it where you want it, hold it in place with your finger, and use a special decal squeegee or a clean, round, synthetic sponge to gently press all the water out from under it. Be sure to remove all water and any air bubbles, or the decal will bubble up during the firing. **3**

Let the decal dry thoroughly before firing. Most decals fire to cone 017, but check the package for any special instructions.

■ CHINA PAINTS

China paint, a very low-firing type of *overglaze*, can be used to provide detailed accents to a leaf **4** or to create more complete images, such as a central flower. **5** For either purpose, premixed china paints are available in a variety of forms, such as tubes, pastes, and semimoist cakes.

All china paints are fired to between cone 018 and cone 015; just follow the manufacturer's instructions.

When firing oil-based paints, it's advisable to prop open the kiln's lid slightly for the first part of the firing, to let out the fumes from evaporating oils and resins. If the kiln is indoors, open the windows or a door, and leave the area until the noxious and often highly toxic fumes have subsided. Use this procedure even if your indoor kiln is vented.

Lusters

Available in opaque metallic gold and silver, and in transparent iridescent colors, lusters offer an entirely different look. A mixture of oil and metallic particles, a luster is applied to a fired glaze surface. In its unfired state, a luster resembles caramelized sugar; once fired, it's transformed into a thin metallic film.

As dazzling as the results can be, great caution should be taken when working with lusters. The fumes from the solvents and oils that suspend the metallic particles are quite hazardous. Wear rubber or latex gloves and work only in a fully ventilated space. Better yet, wear a respirator, especially when working with lusters for long periods of time.

Application must be evenly thin and done in a dust-free atmosphere, because flecks of dust tend to show up after firing, as do brush strokes. Lusters can be thinned with mineral spirits, if necessary, but should never be intermixed, because different metals are not compatible. Dedicate separate brushes for each color, and use them for nothing else.

Lusters are usually fired between cone 022 and cone 018, but follow the manufacturer's recommendations. Follow the safety-conscious firing procedure outlined for china paints, above.

Gallery

Billie Jean Theide
Butte # Czech-4, 1997

3¼ x 9½ x 2¼ inches (8.3 x 24.1 x 5.7 cm)
Slip-cast and altered porcelain; clear glaze cone
15; gas reduction; vintage ceramic decals; low-
fired cone 015; electric fired
Photo by artist

Matt Nolen
Resisting Regret, 2009

34 x 17 x 10 inches (86.4 x 43.2 x 25.4 cm)
Hand-built, white stoneware; slips, stains and
underglaze decoration; cone 6 glaze, electric
kiln; re-fired to cone 04 for laser print transfers;
china paint, luster, decals fired to cone 018
Photo by Caryn Leigh Posnansky

Betsy Rosenmiller
Soup Tureen, 2000

11 x 15½ x 12 inches (27.9 x 39.4 x 30.5 cm)
Cast and hand-built porcelain; cast leaves attached, texture applied with slip trailer; stains and
glazes; electric fired, cone 5; china paint base
colors, cone 018; china paint veins, cone 018
Photos by artist

Kilns and Firing

Without the heat of an oven, a bowl of batter will never make a cake. Without the heat of a kiln, all that clay you just decorated will never become beautiful, durable ceramic ware.

THE SPECULATION IS THAT THE CERAMIC PROCESS WAS FIRST DISCOVERED AT AN ANCIENT CAMPSITE, when someone found a piece of burnt and hardened clay while rummaging around in the ashes. Kilns have evolved greatly since then. There are many different types, categorized by the fuel or energy they use (electric, gas, wood); by a specialized decorating process they're designed for (raku, salt, soda); and by their form or container (beehive, car, pit, barrel). They also come in a wide range of sizes, from electric test kilns the size of a household microwave to mammoth fuel-fired kilns the size of a railroad car.

Set up the kiln away from your workspace if possible. Be sure to vent it to the outdoors, to avoid breathing in the fumes. With a selection of full and half shelves, posts in a variety of sizes, and pyrometric cones, you'll be ready for your first firing.

■ CHOOSING A KILN

A kiln is a significant investment for anyone starting out in clay work.

Many communities have ceramic shops, pottery cooperatives, or community colleges that offer ceramics courses and access to kilns. Some businesses will fire your work for you, usually charging by the cubic foot. If you don't already have a kiln, you might look into these options before you buy. A ceramics class is enormously helpful for a beginner—especially in the realm of kilns and firing.

When you're ready, it's important to buy the right kind of kiln for your particular needs. An electric kiln is the best choice for a beginner. It's the easiest to set up and use, and its clean heat doesn't react with ceramic

materials. Models vary widely in size, in controls (from manual to fully automated), and in price.

Thick, energy-efficient brick walls rated to the temperature you plan to work in are essential. It's also important to keep fumes from the firing out of enclosed workspaces or living

▶ **Tip:** The majority of electric kilns on the market are top loaders, meaning you have to bend over and reach in to load them. If you have a bad back, you might want to look into a front-loading kiln.

areas. Proper ventilation is, therefore, essential. From the several different venting options available, choose the one that best suits your situation. **1**

■ KILN FURNITURE

To pack your kiln with layers of ceramic ware, you'll need *kiln furniture*—shelves, and the posts to separate them. These can be ordered à la cart, though there are kits available that offer a good starter selection of posts and enough shelves to stack two or three levels of ware.

To protect the shelves from glaze drips, one side of each needs to be coated with kiln wash, a powdered mixture of clay and refractory materials such as silica and alumina. Add water, stir the mixture to a light, creamy consistency, and brush on a couple of thin coats—they'll last longer than a single thick one. Dipping the ends of the posts in *kiln wash* helps protect them from sticking as well.

Pieces can touch one another in a bisque firing, but take care that nothing touches the element wires in the walls of the kiln.

■ LOADING THE KILN

When your clay pieces have safely reached the greenware stage—their color has lightened, and you can't feel any dampness when you hold them up to your cheek—it's time to load your kiln for the bisque firing.

Whenever possible, kiln furniture should be stacked using a *tripodic* (three-post) support system, because it's the most stable. Start the first shelf at least ½ inch (1.3 cm) off the kiln floor, supporting it on three short posts. As you add shelves, position the posts over the ones below, up through the entire stack. This helps prevent stresses during firing that might cause the shelves to warp or crack. With each

layer, position your posts on the shelf first, so you know there will be room for them once the ware is loaded. Add the larger, more awkwardly shaped pieces first, and fit the smaller forms around them. Never place furniture or ceramic ware near or touching the elements of an electric kiln. **2**

In the bisque firing, the ware can touch each other. Greenware can be stacked inside and piled upon each other, as long as the ware is sturdy and you follow common sense. Forms such as bowls, plates, cups, and mugs can be stacked rim to rim or foot to foot, as long as they are close in size. Don't place heavy work on delicate pieces, and avoid putting weight on the ware's stress points. (See the illustration on page 116.) **3** Also, don't pack the kiln so densely that you restrict the movement of air and heat. This would give you uneven firing results.

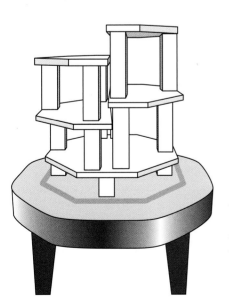

To prevent kiln shelves from cracking, kiln posts need to line up as closely as possible from layer to layer through the entire stack. While three posts per shelf is the ideal, when moving from a whole shelf to half shelves, start with four posts to support the six post points above.

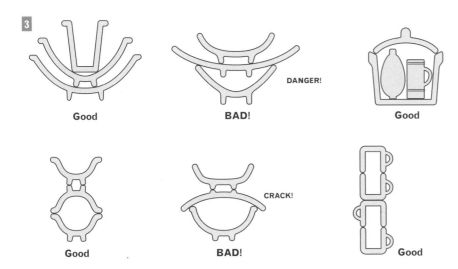

3

Good   BAD! (DANGER!)   Good

Good   BAD! (CRACK!)   Good

In a bisque firing, wide, open forms can be set inside one another, while bowls, plates, and cups may be stacked rim to rim. Just keep the stacks low (no more than three or four pieces) and in groups of similar size.

4

In a glaze firing, pieces may be close but not touching, or else they will permanently fuse together.

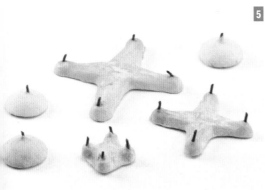

5

Stilts are useful for holding pieces that need to be glazed on all sides.

The glaze firing is a different story. If glazed pieces touch during the firing, they will emerge fused together. They should be no closer than ½ inch (1.3 cm) to each other or to the posts or walls. Check the bottom of each piece before loading, and sponge off any dried glaze drips, to prevent it from fusing to the shelf during firing. **4**

Odd-shaped or sculptural pieces that need to be glazed on all surfaces can be propped up on *stilts*. These ceramic holders are embedded with prongs made from a special refractory wire that leave barely discernible marks in the glaze surface as they keep your ware from touching the kiln shelf. **5**

Last, add your cone packs, positioning them where you can see them through the peepholes. (See "Firing Temperatures and Cones," page 118, and "Cone Packs," page 119.)

■ THE SCIENCE OF FIRING

In the process of firing, clay goes through a series of irreversible physical and chemical changes. A broad understanding of this process will serve you well when you make specific decisions about firing.

In the early stages of the bisque firing, a kiln's temperature must be raised slowly, for several reasons. No matter how dry greenware may seem, it contains a certain amount of atmospheric moisture. Drying is fully completed only during the early stages of firing. Up to the point at which the kiln reaches 212°F (100°C), water in the clay evaporates and is driven off as steam. This evaporation must happen slowly, or the steam will build up inside the ware, perhaps causing it to explode.

Chemically bonded water begins to be driven off at about 660°F (350°C). By the time it reaches 932°F (500°C), an irreversible chemical change in the

The glowing elements of a firing electric kiln. This is for purely illustrative purposes. Do not—I repeat, do not—open a kiln during firing!

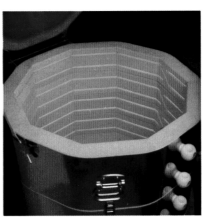

Photo courtesy of Skutt Kilns

clay, known as *dehydration*, takes place. The ware can no longer be dissolved in water and returned to a pliable state.

At the same time, the organic material begins to burn off, beginning with vegetable matter and culminating at about 1652°F (900°C), when all carbon, inorganic carbonates, and sulfates have been oxidized. Be careful as these gasses escape. If the firing proceeds too rapidly, carbon may be trapped within the clay body, resulting in bloated and blackened ware.

Quartz inversion is another critical phase in the firing. At 1063°F (573°C), the quartz crystals in the clay change from alpha to beta forms, and the ware undergoes a slight increase in volume. The transformation reverses itself at the same temperature during the cooling, when beta quartz returns to its alpha form and the ware to its original size. Moving through this stage too quickly, during either heating or cooling, can result in *dunting*—sharp, clean cracks through the ware. **6**

A clean crisp, break such as this one signals that the platter is *dunted*, a defect caused by being heated or cooled too quickly.

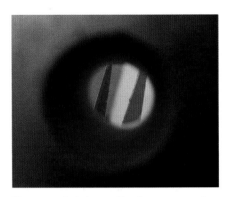

Use a peephole to monitor the progress of the firing.

At this point, a peek into the kiln chamber—through a peephole, of course—would reveal a slight red glow. If your kiln doesn't have a pyrometer, becoming familiar with the kiln chamber color at the various stages of firing is very useful. Check the "Kiln Colors and Firing Stages" chart on page 118; note that most of the critical points of the firing occur before any color is visible in the chamber. This tells you that the temperature should be raised slowly until the kiln has attained a dark red color. After that, the temperature may be increased more quickly.

▶ **Tip:** Exercise caution when you look into the kiln beyond the dark-red-color stage of firing. The bright color of the heat can be damaging to your retina. Wear welding goggles or glasses when you look through a peephole.

Now the gradual progression of ceramic *vitrification* begins. The clay continues this process of hardening and tightening throughout the rest of the firing, until it reaches a mature, or *vitrified*, state of maximum density and durability. In the bisque firing, however, the progression is usually cut short. The clay is purposely under-fired, as a preparation for glazing. You can raise the kiln's temperature more rapidly in the first stages of a glaze firing because most of the critical transformations occurred during the bisque firing—which, depending on the maturing temperature of the clay body, ranges from about 1562°F to 1832°F (850°C to 1000°C), or cone 010 to cone 06. In a glaze firing, the only time you need to be cautious is during quartz inversion.

As the glaze approaches its maturity, it enters the molten stage and begins to bubble. The bubbles gradually smooth out as the firing progresses. If the temperature increases or decreases too abruptly during the molten state, the glaze surface may contain numerous bubbles or pinholes. This can happen even if the cones indicate that the proper temperature has been reached.

For this reason you should *soak* the glaze at the end of the firing, when the desired temperature has been reached. Soaking entails holding the kiln at the target temperature for a period of time to allow the glaze materials to fully melt and even out. The duration of a soak can be anywhere from 10 minutes to an hour, depending on the particular glaze; some are more susceptible to

Kiln Colors and Firing Stages

KILN COLOR	INTERIOR TEMPERATURE/CONE	EFFECT	WARE/GLAZE TYPES
No color	0°–212°F (0°–100°C)	Ware dries; water driven off as steam	
	660°F (350°C)		
	662°–1652°F (350°–900°C)	Chemical water driven off	
Lowest visible red	932°F (500°C)	Organic material burned away (first plant material, then carbon and sulfur)	
	1063°F (573°C)	Dehydration (irreversible chemical change) complete	
	Δ022 – Δ020		
Lowest visible red to dark red	Δ020 – Δ017	Quartz inversion; vitrification process begins	
Dark red to cherry red	Δ017 – Δ015		China paint
			Overglaze enamels
			Lusters
Bright cherry red to orange	Δ015 – Δ010		Decals
Orange to yellow	Δ010 – Δ03		Bisque
			Earthenware
			Terra-cotta
Yellow to light yellow	Δ03 – Δ11		Low-fire glazes
Light yellow to white	Δ11 – Δ20		Mid- to high-range stoneware
			Porcelain

producing bubbles than others are. Experience with specific glazes is your best guide.

To soak the glaze in a manual or semiautomatic kiln, simply set the temperature back to low—don't shut it off—once the kiln reaches the desired temperature. If you're using a computerized or fully automatic kiln, follow the manufacturer's instructions for adding a soaking ramp at the end of the firing.

■ FIRING TEMPERATURES AND CONES

So far, firing temperature has been discussed primarily as a matter of heat alone. However, the maturation of ceramic material is also related to the amount of time it's cooked in the fire. The combination of heat and time, known as *heat work*, brings clay and glazes to full vitrification.

Although mere temperature can be read by a *pyrometer* (an instrument for reading high temperatures), something more akin to the ceramic ware itself is needed to accurately measure the absorption of heat over a period of time. That is when cones come into play.

7

Pyrometric cones come in a full range of temperature ratings. They are slightly angled on the bottom, indicating the angle at which they should be set into the cone pack.

Cones—elongated, three-sided pyramids 1 to 2 inches tall (2.5 to 5.1 cm)—are made of ceramic materials similar in composition to glazes. Loaded into the kiln and fired with the ware, a cone bends or collapses to signal the attainment of a particular firing range. **7**

Cones are made in a numbered series (often accompanied by the symbol Δ), each one with a different composition so that it will collapse when the designated temperature is obtained. Most studio ceramists fire between cone 022 (the low end) and cone 12 (the high end). A cone chart with temperature equivalents is on page 118. Be sure to follow the manufacturer's recommendations.

Glazes have much narrower firing ranges than clay bodies do, so the accuracy of cones is especially vital for successful glaze firings.

Cone Packs

Cone packs let you monitor the progress of a firing. Set them in several different places, to gauge whether your kiln is heating evenly, and make sure you can see them through the peepholes.

To make a cone pack, insert three large cones of adjacent temperatures into a roll of heavily grogged clay, as shown in photo .

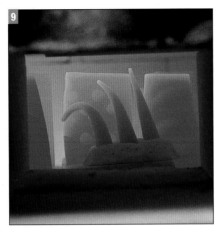

PHOTO BY EVAN BRACKEN

For example, if you want to fire to cone 06, your cones would be 07, 06, and 05. Poke some holes in the clay so that it will dry more quickly. The cones should all face the same way, with the imprinted cone number on the same side, and tilted to the same slight angle. The middle cone is rated for the desired firing temperature and is called the *target cone*. In front of it place the *guide cone* of the next-lower temperature, whose bending will alert you that the kiln is about to attain the maximum desired temperature. If the *guard cone* bends during firing, it indicates that the kiln has exceeded the desired temperature. Manufacturers provide detailed information about how to use cones, so be sure to follow their guidelines. 9

When you embed the cones in a cone pack, face the cones in the direction, and at the angle, indicated by their shape. You should have three consecutive cones in order of increasing temperature: a guide cone, the target cone, and a guard cone.

◼ FIRING PROCEDURE

Begin the firing with all peepholes open. To ensure that the temperature rises slowly and that moisture and gasses can escape during the first part of a bisque firing, prop open the lid 1 or 2 inches (2.5 to 5.1 cm). Use a brick, a piece of kiln furniture, or the bar that is built into some kilns for this purpose.

Check the kiln's manual for specific instructions for increasing the temperature to low, medium, and high settings. Some kilns have controls with additional increments within each of these ranges, allowing for an even more gradual increase in temperature.

Fire the kiln on low heat for four to six hours for a bisque firing, two to three hours for a glaze firing, taking into consideration the thickness of the ware. After this initial period, shut the lid and set the kiln on medium for another two hours, for both bisque and glaze firings. Leave the peepholes open until the kiln has passed the red-heat stage, then reset the kiln to the high temperature setting until it reaches the target temperature. The target temperature for low-fire bisque is usually cone 010 to 08, depending on the clay body. For a glaze firing, the label on the glaze jar will list the target cone, as will any formula you may be working with. (See, for example, "Recipes," page 122.)

Manual and semiautomatic kilns are often equipped with automatic shutoff devices. They are good backups, but don't depend on them completely. They may not be accurate or, worse yet, may fail altogether, causing disastrous damage to your ware, your kiln, or possibly your workspace or home. Even with fully automated, computerized kilns, do not leave the kiln unattended during the firing. Be especially vigilant toward the end of the firing, to make sure the unit has shut off.

Depending on kiln size and load density, it may take another six to 10 hours to reach the desired temperature at the high setting. After four hours of firing on high, check the kiln more frequently. This is especially important for a glaze firing. If you're planning to soak the glaze, turn the kiln back to the low setting when your target cone is *beginning* to bend, rather than when it has fully slumped. Soak for 10 to 45 minutes, checking often for any changes in the target cone. If the soaking period temperature gets too low and the cone hasn't bent to the recommended angle yet, set the temperature a bit higher for a few more minutes. Follow the cone manufacturer's recommendations for firing, or refer to the cone chart on page 118.

If the target cone melts before the automatic shutoff is triggered, then you can manually shut off your kiln. Likewise, if the automatic shutoff ends the firing before the cone melts, turn the kiln back on and vigilantly watch it until the cone has slumped.

Once the kiln is off, let it cool for at least 10 to 12 hours before opening the peepholes. Within three or four hours after that, you can start to prop up the kiln lid, slowly increasing the height from a sliver to 1, 2, and 4 inches

A kiln shelf maintenance kit: a cold chisel for chipping off stubborn glaze drips, a grinding stone for taking off loose kiln wash and debris, and a tub of kiln wash and a brush to recoat the shelf's surface.

(2.5, 5.1, and 10.2 cm). When you can comfortably hold your hand at the lid opening for a minute or two, then open it fully. As your pieces become cool enough to handle, remove them layer by layer. Use kiln gloves or heavy-duty leather work gloves to handle the warm ware.

■ KILN MAINTENANCE

Upon unloading, the kiln should be vacuumed to remove any debris from the kiln floor and the elements. Check the kiln shelves for fired glaze spills. They should be ground or chipped off with a grinding stone or cold chisel, after which a fresh layer of kiln wash needs to be applied. **10**

■ ALTERNATIVE FIRING TECHNIQUES

There is no denying that for many ceramists, part of the allure of ceramics is the chance to work with fire. If you've ever gazed, mesmerized, into the flames of a campfire or fireplace, you might want to look into a couple of alternative, low-fire firing techniques to satisfy that fixation.

Pit and Barrel Firing

Pit and barrel firings are primitive outdoor techniques, fueled by burning wood and sawdust. For pit firing, a hole is dug in the ground; for barrel firing, a 55-gallon (208 l) steel drum is cut in

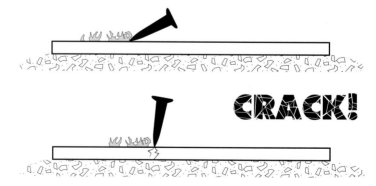

Passing a grinding stone over the kiln shelf may be sufficient in most cases, but stubborn drops of glaze will need to be chiseled off. To do this, hold the cold chisel over the spot at an oblique angle and tap the end gently with a hammer. Be careful: hitting a chisel held at too high an angle could cause the shelf to crack.

half. Wood and ware are carefully piled on top of each other, with a sprinkling of sawdust and straw, and set ablaze. After the initial blaze, the fire is allowed to smolder. Proper placement in the kiln and a bit of luck will leave the ware beautifully marked by smoke, sometimes completely blackened. A terra sigillata surface (see page 69) is especially receptive to the markings of smoke. Striking effects can be had with the addition of oxides to the surface, or by wrapping the ware in copper wire. The pieces need to be fired to a low bisque temperature beforehand, about cone 010, to be able to take the thermal shock this firing can inflict.

If you live in a remote area, you might be able to try this kind of

Pit firings are probably outgrowths of the communal campfire, which is perhaps where the first piece of fired clay was discovered.
Photo by Evan Bracken

firing—but only after you check the local ordinances and current advisories about open fires. You don't want the fire department showing up at your door with a citation and fine—or, far worse, start a fire that gets out of control.

Barrel firings produce results similar to pit firings, but offer a slightly more controllable firing and a larger capacity.
Photo by Evan Bracken

Courtesy of David Jones and the Crowood Press

Raku

An ancient firing process dating back to sixteenth-century Japan, raku is another fire lover's dream. A substantial firing chamber is generally fueled by gas or propane, allowing it to reach glaze-melting temperatures. Results are immediate, because the ware is quickly brought up to temperature, usually in less than an hour. When the glaze has reached maturing temperature, the flame is extinguished, the kiln is opened, and the ware removed while still molten hot. (Special tongs and protective gear are required.) The pieces are then put into a barrel with combustible materials and covered with a metal lid, where they smolder, and the glaze goes through a transformation. It's all quite

dramatic. The specially formulated glazes often produce dazzling metallic effects. Because of the thermal shock the ware endures, special raku clay bodies and glazes must be used. It's not a technique for the lone beginner. If you're curious, seek out classes or workshops at a local school, community college, or potters' group.

Raku firing is in a category all its own. Special clay, glazes, and kiln are required.
Photo by Nicki Pardo

Recipes

These recipes are given in percentages that add up to 100 so you can easily calculate percentages of added colorants. Always use safety precautions (see page 21) when mixing.

■ WHITE WET WARE SLIP

Apply to wet ware or leather hard

Fire cone 04 to cone 01

For colored slip, add 10 to 20 percent stain, depending on how dark the stain is and the intensity of color you desire. For coloring with oxides, use the glaze-coloring guide below as a start; lean toward the higher quantities.

OM4 ball clay	45
Talc	25
Nepheline syenite	20
Edgar Plastic Kaolin	5
Frit 3124	5
Total	100
Zircopax	2

■ CLEAR GLOSS GLAZE

Fire to cone 04 and use a thin application

Frit 3195	89.5
OM4 ball clay	9.5
Magnesium carbonate	1.0
Total	100.0

■ VITREOUS SLIP BASE

Apply to wet ware or leather hard

Fire cone 04 to cone 1

Frit 3110	33
Tile 6 clay	27
Edgar Plastic Kaolin	13
Talc	10
Nepheline syenite	10
Frit 3124	7
Total	100

Thoroughly dry mix a large batch of the base formula. Add colorants to a portion of the base, as needed for the project. For white, add 10 percent Zircopax; for colors, add 20 percent stain.

■ CLEAR MATTE GLAZE

Fire to cone 04 and use a thin application for clear, and a thicker one for translucent, especially when used as a base for colors

Frit 3247	35.6
Gerstley borate	11.9
Kona F-4	33.6
Whiting	12.8
Zinc	3.9
Bentonite	2.0
Magnesium carbonate	0.2
Total	100

■ BASE GLAZE COLORANTS

Once you've found a glaze you like, extend your palette by adding different colorants to it. You can start with any base glaze, be it clear, translucent, opaque, or gloss, textured or matte. If it's already a colored glaze, simply turn it into a base glaze by eliminating the coloring oxide or stain.

Below is a basic guide for how much colorant to add to a base glaze. For even greater variety, feel free to try combinations of oxides with each other or with stains. Glazes react differently to colorants depending on their composition, so always test the mixture before using it on a finished piece.

Stains

DARK-COLORED STAINS, use 8 to 10 percent

LIGHT-COLORED STAINS, use 12 to 15 percent

Coloring Oxides

MEDIUM TO STRONG BLUE, use cobalt carbonate 0.5 to 1 percent

LIGHT TO STRONG GREEN, use copper carbonate 2 to 8 percent

TAN TO DARK BROWN, use iron oxide 4 to 8 percent

MEDIUM TO DARK PURPLE OR PURPLISH, use manganese carbonate 3 to 6 percent

GREEN, use chrome oxide 2 percent

TAN, use rutile 5 percent

GREENISH GRAY OR BROWN, use nickel oxide 2 to 3 percent

GRAY, use iron chromate 2 percent

■ MAJOLICA OPAQUE WHITE GLAZE

Fire to cone 04

Frit 3124	70.4
Edgar Plastic Kaolin	10.0
Strontium carbonate	2.5
Zircopax	17.1
Total	100
Yellow stain	0.25
Rutile	0.25

■ USING COLORING OXIDES AND STAINS AS MAJOLICA DECORATING COLORS

Measure 40 to 50 percent stain or coloring oxide to 50 to 60 percent Frit 3124 or other glaze flux. Some colors may need more or less flux than others. Use the information here as a starting point; test your mixtures before using them and adjust the amount of flux as needed.

If you're using gerstley borate (or a comparable substitute) as the flux, the proportions should be 20 to 25 percent stain or coloring oxide to 75 to 80 percent gerstley borate. Add water and a small quantity of commercial gum solution to the dry mixture. (If you prefer to mix your own, see "Gum Solution," page 124.)

Many coloring oxides, such as copper carbonate, cobalt oxide, and manganese carbonate, don't need flux. Mix them only with water and gum solution. Finally, add 60 percent or more flux to more refractory oxides, such as chrome oxide and rutile.

■ TERRA SIGILLATA

Make terra sigillata by mixing any clay or combination of clays with water and a suspension agent (a deflocculant) such as sodium silicate, Darvan, or TSP. (TSP stands for trisodium phosphate, a cleaning agent that's available from the paint department of hardware stores.) Clays with finer particles will produce a larger amount of terra sigillata. Keep in mind that you must mix terra sigillata with clay that's suitable for the firing temperature range of your clay body. Store the deflocculated slip in a 1-gallon (3.8 l) glass jar.

Basic Terra Sigillata

This consists of a 7:3 ratio of water to clay, plus some deflocculant.

Water	3.4 liters (14 cups)
Clay or clay mixture	*1,500 grams (3.3 pounds)
Deflocculant	7.5 grams (1 level teaspoon)

*For terra sigillata with natural clay color, use the appropriate clay type:

Buff terra sigillata	100 percent Goldart
Red-brown terra sigillata	100 percent Redart
Light orange terra sigillata	50 percent Redart plus 50 percent ball clay

White Terra Sigillata

Fire cone 04 to cone 01. For cone 01 and higher, use 100 percent ball clay, EPK, or a mixture of the two.

Some types of white clay, including EPK and ball clay, are too refractory to use in a lower-temperature terra sigillata; in such cases, a special formula is needed.

Water	3.4 liters (14 cups)
OM 4 ball clay	600 grams (1.3 pounds)
Talc	450 grams (1 pound)
Edgar Plastic Kaolin	225 grams (0.5 pound)
Zircopax	150 grams (0.3 pound)
Deflocculant	7.5 grams (1 level teaspoon)

For a large batch of colored terra sigillata, add 225 grams of stain to the dry base recipe and proceed as usual. For smaller batches, add 3 to 10 percent commercial stains or oxides to a 100-gram batch of the finished terra sigillata, but only 0.5 to 1 percent cobalt oxide or carbonate.

Continued on next page

Rich Black Terra Sigillata

Fire cone 04 to cone 02

Water	1.2 liters (5 cups)
Redart	500 grams (1.1 pounds)
Black copper oxide	25 grams (4 teaspoons)
Cobalt carbonate	50 grams (8 teaspoons)
Manganese dioxide	25 grams (4 teaspoons)
Deflocculant	7.5 grams (1 level teaspoon)

■ GUM SOLUTION

I recommend beginners simply buy a jar of commercially prepared gum solution; you're not likely to quickly use the quantities that this recipe makes, much less use up a pound, the common minimum unit it's sold in. Several different types of gum exist on the market; some are powdered, while others come in flake form. The flakes can be difficult to mix, and gums, as organic materials, tend to break down and spoil. However, I've found CMC (carboxymethylcellulose) powder to provide the best results for this procedure.

Using an electric beater, work 8 ounces (236.6 ml) of rubbing alcohol into 3½ ounces (100 grams) of CMC powder until the powder becomes mushy. Continue beating while adding 72 ounces (2 l) of very hot water. The resulting syrup can be added to glazes or slips as a binder, thickener, or suspension agent in quantities ranging from ½ to 1 cup (118.3 to 236.6 ml) per 1 gallon (3.8 l). Add the solution in small quantities until you arrive at the results you desire.

Glossary

Bisque. Ceramic ware that's been fired to between cone 010 and cone 06. A bisque firing prepares the ware for glazing and subsequent glaze firing.

Blistering. A glaze defect that presents itself as bubbles or craters that result from burst bubbles that are left behind on the surface when the glaze hasn't had time to smooth out before it cools and sets.

Ceramic. Clay that's been fired, causing it to undergo a permanent chemical conversion that makes the material strong and stable.

Ceramic decals. Images silk-screened onto a decal carrier paper using specially formulated china paints, and applied to fired glaze surfaces. The ware is then refired to a lower temperature, usually around cone 018 to 016.

Ceramic stain. A chemically stable ceramic coloring agent formulated from a combination of coloring oxides, alumina, flint, and a fluxing agent. The mixture is calcined (fired), finely ground, and washed for use in glazes for overglaze and underglaze decoration and for clay body colorants.

Clay body. A combination of clay ingredients formulated to mature at a desired temperature and to have certain working or color characteristics.

Coloring oxides. Raw ceramic materials used to impart color to glazes, slips, or clay bodies.

Cone. A cone-shaped ceramic material rated according to its ability to melt. The precise combination of time and rate of temperature change needed to melt it is indicated by a number between 022 and 12. Also called pyrometric cones, cones are often represented by the delta symbol (Δ).

Crawling. A glaze defect that happens during the melting process when the glaze cracks and pulls apart, roll back on itself, leaving bare spots of exposed clay.

Crazing. A glaze defect characterized by a network of fine cracks. It's caused by an improper fit of glaze that's in tension with the clay.

Deflocculant. A soluble material added to slips to increase fluidity. They're also used to disperse the fine clay particle of a clay suspension when making terra sigillata.

Flux. A low-melting compound or oxide found in a glaze or clay that promotes glass formation by interacting with the other ingredients during the firing, enabling them to fuse into a hard, permanent, and impervious ceramic product.

Greenware. Dried, unfired ceramic ware.

Gum solution. A solution of natural gums used in glazes as a binder to improve the flow and brushability of glaze. Gum also promotes better glaze adherence to the body; the material called CMC is used as a gum substitute.

Kiln. A high-temperature furnace made of refractory and insulating materials, for firing ceramic ware. Its heat source is electricity or gas or other combustible materials.

Kiln furniture. Shelves, posts, and stilts made of refractory material and used to support ware in the kiln.

Kiln wash. A mixture of clay and other refractory materials like silica and alumina, used on kiln furniture as a protective coating against accidental drips from melting glaze during the firing.

Leather hard. Clay that has dried sufficiently to be stiff but is still damp enough to carve or to be joined to other clay pieces with slip.

Low fire. Describes low-temperature clays and glazes that mature at ranges lower than cone 04.

Luster. A metallic decoration applied to glazed and fired surfaces as a thin metallic film, which is a mixture of resins and metallic particles. The ware is refired to between cone 022 and 014.

Majolica. A glazing technique in which an unfired opaque white glaze surface is decorated with coloring oxides or stains. Typically associated with low-fire earthenware, majolica technique can be fired at any other temperature.

Overglaze. A ceramic or metallic decoration applied and low fired (between cone 018 and 013) on a previously glazed surface.

Oxide. A chemical combination of oxygen with another metal or nonmetal element. Coloring oxides are metal oxides that impart color to the fired ceramic material.

Pinholing. A glaze defect that develops when air bubbles in the molten glaze burst and don't have time to heal, leaving behind a network of tiny holes or pits in the glaze surface.

Refractory materials. Materials resistant to high temperatures.

Sgraffito. Decoration achieved by scratching through a colored slip or stain to reveal the contrasting body or glaze color underneath it.

Sieve. A bowl or frame with fine mesh across the bottom, used for sifting slips and glazes to create a uniform mixture and eliminate unwanted coarse particles.

Slip. Clay in liquid suspension used to join clay pieces. Slip can be made from a working clay body or formulated for decorative purposes.

Slip trailing. A decorative technique in which a plastic squeeze bottle is used to extrude a thin trail of slip or glaze onto ceramic ware.

Sprig. A surface decoration that's added to the surface of the main form as a relief. A sprig is often formed using a sprig mold, but a hand-formed clay appliqué may be referred to as a sprig as well.

Stain. A stable coloring agent made up of one or more coloring oxides together with alumina, flint, and a fluxing compound. Stain is used to color glazes, overglazes, underglazes, and clay bodies.

Terra sigillata. A glazelike slip decanted from the finest particles of clay. After application to greenware or bisque, its surface is burnished or polished with a smooth, hard object or chamois for a waxed-looking surface.

Underglaze. A colored decoration applied to bisque or greenware and usually covered with a glaze before firing.

Vitreous. Describes the hard, glassy, and nonabsorbent quality of a clay body or glaze.

Vitreous slip. A decorating slip with sufficient flux to provide a durable surface with saturated color.

Vitrification. The hardest state to which a clay body can be fired without deformation. At this stage, glass forms and the body strengthens and shrinks somewhat.

Wax resist. A melted wax or wax emulsion applied to ware prior to decorating to prevent slips or glazes from adhering to the protected areas. It can be applied to raw or bisque ware, over a glaze or between two layers of it.

Wet ware. Wet clay that's been formed into an object but hasn't yet begun to dry.

Acknowledgments

I'D LIKE TO THANK ALL THOSE PERSONS, throughout my schooling and career, who have so generously shared their knowledge with me, whether in person, in video or in print, as teacher, colleague, or student.

I'd like especially to acknowledge my very first ceramic teacher, Ken Vavrek, at Moore College of Art, whose creative projects inspired me to switch majors from painting to ceramics. I'm also grateful to the teachers who followed—namely Val Cushing, Wayne Higby, and Bill Parry (posthumously) at Alfred University, from which I graduated with a BFA in ceramics; and John Stephenson and Georgette Zirbes at the University of Michigan, where I received my MFA in ceramics.

Many others have added to this solid base by sharing their expertise and tips, and I owe them gratitude as well. One of the most recent that I'd like to note is Posey Bacopoulus, who gave me majolica tips during the summer of 2009 while we were both teaching at Penland School of Crafts. It was so nice to have gotten to know you!

I wish to thank Suzanne Tourtillott for initially inviting me to author this book. I'd further like to extend my most gracious thanks to the remarkable cast of characters who helped me the rest of the way through; they are editor Nathalie Mornu, who kept the ball rolling; copy editor Carol Taylor, who made sense of it all; and editorial assistant Kathleen McCafferty, who took care of the details.

Of course, a most hearty thanks to Dan Milner, the best photographer a how-to book-writing gal could ask for. Thanks for being wonderful to work with, a great photographer and friend.

Finally, I thank all the artists who responded to my request for imagery and who so generously prepared and submitted photos of their pieces for this book. Alas, there wasn't enough room to fit all of the wonderful artwork I would have liked to include.

About the Author

Angelica Pozo, a studio artist living and working in Cleveland, Ohio, has been a visiting instructor at schools including the Cleveland Institute of Art and the Penn State School of Visual Arts. Her workshop and artist residency credits include the Tile Heritage Conference at the Erie Art Museum, Arrowmont School of Arts and Crafts, Haystack Mountain School of Crafts, Penland School of Crafts, Southwest School of Art & Craft, Manchester Craftsmen's Guild, and Baltimore Clayworks.

Ms. Pozo has received many awards, including an Ohio Arts Council Individual Artist Fellowship. Her work is featured in a number of permanent collections, including the Museum of Arts and Design in New York and the National Afro-American Museum & Cultural Center in Wilberforce, Ohio. Her site-specific public art is installed at various public institutions in Ohio. Her studio work has been featured in numerous solo and group exhibitions. Ms. Pozo is the author of *Making and Installing Handmade Tiles* (Lark, 2005). Her writing and art were also featured in *The Penland Book of Ceramics: Master Classes in Ceramic Techniques* (Lark, 2003).

Contributing Artists

Index

CERAMICS FOR BEGINNERS

OTHER BOOKS IN THIS SERIES

Hand Building

by Shay Amber

A beginner's workshop reveals the unlimited possibilities of hand building. With Shay Amber's simple and basic approach to hand building, you can learn how to make both sculptural and useful forms. She shares fundamental techniques and 12 projects to practice them on, including a Coiled Bottle, Wall Pocket, Carved Lantern, Appliqué Tile, and a Square Plate. Amber also introduces you to surface decoration and glaze treatments. In addition, you'll find inspiring gallery selections highlighting other artists' work.

Shay Amber is a ceramic artist living in Asheville, North Carolina, who works exclusively with hand-built forms. She holds a degree in ceramics from Ringling School of Art and Design, completed a three-year residency at Odyssey Center for the Ceramic Arts, and received a scholarship to Watershed Center for the Ceramic Arts. Her work is displayed in galleries and permanent collections nationally.

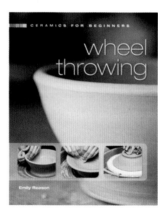

Wheel Throwing

by Emily Reason

Master the fundamentals while creating beautiful ceramic pieces. Follow along with Emily Reason as she teaches you wheel throwing, one skill at a time. She makes it easy to learn basic techniques like throwing a cylinder and pulling a handle, and will guide you step-by-step as you create attractive projects ranging from a mug and a pitcher to a teapot and tulipiere. Every project includes a list of the tools you'll need to make it, easy-to-follow instructions, and detailed how-to photographs.

Emily Reason is a full-time potter and teacher who specializes in functional pottery. Her work has been exhibited at the Philadelphia Museum Craft Show; the Smithsonian Craft Show; the annual conference of the National Council on Education for the Ceramic Arts (NCECA); the Society for Contemporary Craft in Pittsburgh, Pennsylvania; and has been published in Ceramics Monthly.